Management Extra

INFORMATION AND KNOWLEDGE MANAGEMENT

Management Extra

INFORMATION AND KNOWLEDGE MANAGEMENT

ELSEVIER

eLEARN

Pergamon
Flexible
Learning

AMSTERDAM • BOSTON • HEIDELBERG • LONDON • NEW YORK • OXFORD • PARIS •
SAN DIEGO • SAN FRANCISCO • SINGAPORE • SYDNEY • TOKYO

Elsevier Butterworth-Heinemann
Linacre House, Jordan Hill, Oxford OX2 8DP
30 Corporate Drive, Burlington, MA 01803

First published 2005

British Library Cataloguing in Publication Data
A catalogue record for this book is available from the British Library

Library of Congress Cataloguing in Publication Data
A catalogue record for this book is available from the Library of Congress

ISBN 0 7506 6688 9

For information on all Elsevier Butterworth-Heinemann publications
visit our website at www.books.elsevier.com

Printed and bound in Italy

Contents

Activities

Figures

Tables

Series Preface

*'I hear I forget
I see I remember
I do I understand'*

Galileo

Management Extra is designed to help you put ideas into practice. Each book in the series is full of thought-provoking ideas, examples and theories to help you understand the key management concepts of our time. There are also activities to help you see how the concepts work in practice.

The text and activities are organised into bite-sized themes or topics. You may want to review a theme at a time, concentrate on gaining understanding through the text or focus on the activities whilst dipping into the text for reference.

The activities are varied. Some are work-based, asking you to consider changing, developing and extending your current practice. Others ask you to reflect on new ideas, check your understanding or assess the application of concepts in different contexts. The activities will give you a valuable opportunity to practise various techniques in a safe environment.

And, finally, exploring and sharing your ideas with others can be very valuable in making the most of this resource.

More information on using this book as part of a course or programme of learning is available on the Management Extra website.

www.managementextra.co.uk

Information is crucial

Information is so crucial to all aspects of our lives that we literally cannot afford to manage it badly. Individuals and organisations rely on their ability to select and process information, both to make sense of their local environment and to try to understand the bigger picture. Information management underpins the key activities of planning, analysis, action and, above all, learning and development.

How to make information useful

Organisations need to manage information well and consistently in order to be responsive to the needs of their customers. This book approaches information management from two key perspectives:

- How you as a manager use and manage information
- The information management process and how it impacts on decision making and organisational performance.

It looks at information in five themes, starting with the sourcing of information and culminating in an exploration of the ways in which organisations manage information and knowledge.

Finding information to meet your needs –
finding good sources of information

Managing your incoming information –
reducing the overload

Managing your outgoing information –
the way you communicate information

How organisations manage information and knowledge –
the systems

How organisations manage information and knowledge –
the content

Your objectives are to:

- Identify sources of information relevant to your needs inside and outside of your organisation

- Evaluate and improve the quality of your information sources

- Learn how to manage information overload

- Describe key principles for communicating effectively in writing

- Identify the principles behind information system design and management

- Explain the features of knowledge management.

1 Information and decision making

People need information to plan their work, meet their deadlines and achieve their goals. They need it to analyse problems and make decisions. Information is certainly not in short supply these days, but not all of it is useful or reliable. This first theme explores your needs for information and asks you to consider how they are served by the sources of information that are available to you.

In this theme you will:

◆ **Consider the differences between data, information and knowledge**

◆ **Identify and evaluate the sources of information that you use**

◆ **Assess whether information flows effectively within your team and identify areas for improvement**

◆ **Analyse how effectively you use the Internet as an information source.**

From data to information to knowledge and learning

H D Clifton (1990) wrote that 'one man's information is another man's data', and certainly the definitions are blurred. However, it is now generally agreed that 'data' is pure and unprocessed – facts and figures without any added interpretation or analysis. Depending on the context, data can be highly significant. Think of a cricket or football score, your name and address. Since it provides the raw material to build information, it also has to be accurate. Any inaccuracies within the initial raw data will magnify as they aggregate upwards, and will seriously corrupt the validity of any conclusions you draw from it or decisions you base upon it.

Data

In a business context, data is associated with the operational aspects of the business and its day-to-day running. As such, it is often entered into a system and stored in large quantities, for example payroll data and sales figures. Such input data goes to create a data 'set' – names and addresses for a mail-merge file, an index to an online product database. It has to be structured correctly – all systems have some kind of validation process to check for obvious technical errors and missing data. To be reliable, the content needs to be accurate, not simply in terms of the correct number and type of characters per data field, but what the data actually represents in terms of meaning. This needs human intervention. Another aspect that affects accuracy is where the data comes from. You may be able to check your own in-house sources – for example, for internally generated data such as the payroll – but have to depend on trust (or the reputation of the supplier) for data received from outside, for example customer credit card details.

Information

So how does 'data' (whether internal or external) become 'information'? When it is applied to some purpose and is adding value which has meaning for the recipient, for example taking sets of sales figures (data) and producing a sales report on them (information).

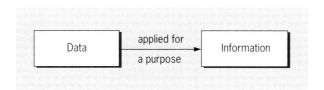

Figure 1.1 *From data to information*

Of course, the same set of data can be used to produce different kinds of information, depending on how it is applied and who applies it. The same sales figures that you use to produce a market sector report might be used by someone else to justify adding to or reducing the size of the sales team. Such information can be used to manage a department, and for short and medium-term planning. Data can move to information and be turned to practical advantage very quickly – in 1815 the London Stock Market rapidly took advantage of the news brought by carrier pigeon of Wellington's victory at Waterloo, which arrived two days before the human messenger arrived.

Information produced inside the organisation can be supplemented by a wealth of business information produced outside – market analyses, reports and case studies, for example.

Put briefly, information by itself is only of use if it is:

◆ the right information (fit for the purpose)

◆ at the right time

◆ in the right format

◆ at the right price.

Knowledge

Just as the words 'data' and 'information' are used interchangeably, there is considerable blurring and confusion between the terms 'information' and 'knowledge'. It is helpful to think of knowledge as being of two types: the instinctive, subconscious, tacit or hidden knowledge, and the more formal, explicit or publicly available knowledge. An everyday example of these might be the knowledge that you use when driving a car (tacit), compared with the knowledge available from a driving manual or the Highway Code (explicit).

Theme 5 looks at knowledge in more detail and how it can be managed within organisations.

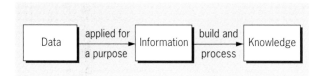

Figure 1.2 *From data to information to knowledge*

In a business context, knowledge is often linked to strategic levels of management and long-term business planning, where it is associated with having a head for business or business flair. However, knowledge vital to an organisation's success can come from any level within it, and needs to be recognised as an important part of organisational assets. It combines information, experience and insight into a mix that is unique to every employee. It is this mix of understandings, based on personal knowledge at a tacit level, that creates the strengths and at times the vulnerability of organisations. It is important for organisations to recognise that holding knowledge at the tacit or hidden level can only have value where people are isolated from everyone else in their decision making. This is neither realistic nor good business practice.

Let's sum up data–information–knowledge with an everyday example. Assume that you're trying to decide on a specialist holiday for photography enthusiasts. Here, very broadly, are the stages you will go through:

Stage 1: collect lots of brochures on photography holidays. This is your basic data store.

Stage 2: work through the brochures, filtering out what you don't want by applying your own criteria to them. Some will be in places you don't want to go to, or at the wrong time of year, or the programmes may be at the wrong level of expertise (you may be looking for some advanced tuition, and many of the holidays are geared to beginners). You can now apply your information and make a decision on where to go on your holiday.

Stage 3: you go on your holiday and build your knowledge from testing your actual experience of the holiday against the information you had when you booked it. This knowledge (which you can use next time you want a similar holiday) can be kept to yourself (tacit) or you can share it by reporting back to your local photography club (explicit).

Capitalising on knowledge by making the tacit explicit, and identifying and managing the processes that nurture it, is a thread that runs through this book.

Building knowledge – learning

So how do we collect, process and build our knowledge? Kolb (1985) believes that there are four stages we all go through as part of the learning cycle:

◆ learning from feeling (through specific experience and relations with other people)

◆ learning by watching and listening (looking at things from different perspectives, observing carefully and reflecting before making judgements)

◆ learning by thinking (reflecting on and analysing ideas, drawing up mental maps and planning)

◆ learning by doing (getting things done, influencing other people, taking risks).

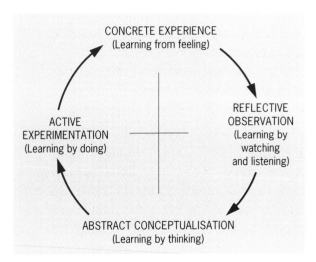

Figure 1.3 *Kolb's learning cycle*   Source: *Kolb* (1985)

We all go through each of these processes to an extent, but different people feel more comfortable with some than with others. For example, an action-oriented person who likes to learn by doing may get very frustrated in a learning-by-watching situation or in one that requires reflection and analysis. It is useful for managers to be aware of their own and their staff's learning styles, since these provide valuable insights into making most effective use of different methods of training.

Argyris and Schön (1974) argue that people act in accordance with a set of mental maps that they themselves have created. It is these subconscious maps (or private, self-generated theories) that guide people's actions. They called these theories that are implicit in what we do theories-in-use: these are what govern our actual behaviour. The words we use to describe that behaviour to others – how we like to justify our actions to other people, or what we would like them to think – can be quite different. This is called espoused theory. It may sound cynical, but if someone asks you how you would behave in a particular set of circumstances, the answer you will give will almost certainly be espoused theory: the public rather than the private set of principles.

Argyris and Schön's view is that real effectiveness results from developing congruence between theory-in-use and espoused theory: creating harmony between your inner and outer self.

Theme 5 looks at a theory-in-use model and the options for organisational learning.

Learning – from the individual to the organisation

People learn by seeking out information when faced with a new situation, and using this information to draw conclusions and form mental models which they use as the basis for their action. If these mental models are confirmed and reinforced by our experience in reality, then over time they become so familiar that they become routine, used automatically and with no conscious effort.

This applies to the presenter who always opens up proceedings with a joke. It also applies to the air traffic controller at an international airport, but in this case we expect the knowledge to be embedded and made explicit through a series of rules and procedures that are recognised and shared by everyone else.

Organisations use routines, rules and procedures as a way of sharing knowledge and creating standardised processes throughout the organisation. These are the systems we use to do our work. Such systems existed before the desktop computer, but computerisation has led to sophisticated information technology (IT) systems for accessing, inputting, processing and sharing information that can be used widely and quickly across the organisation.

The problem for organisations is that routines become old learning and so embedded into our systems that they stifle creativity and the flexibility to respond to changing circumstances. This flexibility – the ability to change and learn – is essential to organisations if they are to survive and grow. The way organisations seek to encourage learning and the sharing of information and knowledge are important aspects of information management.

Activity 1

Identify the differences between data and information

Objectives

This activity will help you to:

◆ check your understanding of data, information and knowledge

◆ identify how you add value to data and information to serve your purpose and create knowledge.

Task

1 List six items of data or information that you receive regularly.

2 Categorise each as 'data' or 'information'.

3 Summarise what you use each item for – your purpose.

4 Note how you add value to each item to create information or knowledge.

5 Who is involved in this process?

Item of data/ information?	Data or information	Purpose	How you add value	Who is involved in adding value?

Feedback

Your work on this activity should have given you some insight into the fact that data on its own is of limited value, and that value has to be added to it to turn it into information. However, the key value-added is knowledge. Use this activity to gain a deeper appreciation of the knowledge available in yourself and your colleagues.

Information comes in many forms

Here are just a few reasons why you, as a manager, need information:

- ◆ You need to understand what the organisation as a whole is doing, as well as understand what is happening in your own unit or department

- ◆ You need to be aware of wider industry developments that may impact on the business

- ◆ It helps day-to-day problem solving and longer-term planning

- ◆ It can avoid having to reinvent the wheel

- ◆ Being aware of different practices and other ways of doing things can spark off new ideas and facilitate change.

You use information all the time, often unconsciously. It comes in many different forms, and these are explained here.

Forms of information

Forms of information include the following:

- ◆ **Internal and external** – information generated inside the organisation and information generated outside. External intelligence and research may be incorporated into internal reports, and issues arising from internal reports may stimulate external market research.

> **Information need not be written down or be verbalised to be valuable**

- ◆ **Electronic and hard copy (paper-based), and spoken.** At Sun Microsystems, employees receive, on average, 100 e-mails each day, but few people work in a paperless office. Most people also use conversation with others for information.

7

- **Hard and soft** – or quantitative and qualitative. Hard information is often derived from large quantities of precise factual data, such as figures, that lends themselves to statistical analysis. Soft information, on the other hand, tends to come from few sources and depends on opinions, feelings, impressions and judgements.

- **Formal and informal.** This is worth exploring in more depth.

Formal and informal

Some of the **formal** information sources you might use every day include:

- newspapers or electronic newsfeeds

- magazine articles

- management reports

- staff disciplinary procedures

- videos of product presentations

- layouts, maps, blueprints.

You will also use a number of **informal** information sources – so informal that you might not even recognise them as such! They can include:

- a chat with the managing director's personal assistant whilst queuing for lunch

- checking out a problem with a colleague

- meeting up with colleagues from the same trade or professional association at the annual conference

- informal contacts with suppliers and customers.

Some of the most useful of these sources will be information gatekeepers – people who routinely collect, evaluate and disseminate information in an informal way which may have nothing to do with their job role. These people are well aware of the way information flows around their local environment, and can exercise an influence that goes well beyond their notional status within the organisation.

If you think about it, information need not even be written down or verbalised to be valuable. You can learn a lot about an organisation and its culture simply by walking about and keeping your eyes open, observing the way the organisation goes about its business and presents itself to staff and the outside world.

There are some key differences in the characteristics of formal and informal information sources, as shown in Table 1.1.

Formal	Informal
Available to more than one person	May be an interchange between just two people
Information captured has been recorded in some way, so can be reused	The information is transient – not stored or retrievable
The information used is selected by the recipient – for example, you decide which newspaper reports you are going to read	The information is selected by the provider
Information tends to be static	Information is interactive
Information is likely to conform to the organisation's promoted self-image – it is likely to be 'espoused theory'	Information is more likely to be 'private' and although partial, is likely to be closer to theory-in-use than formal information sources

Table 1.1 *Characteristics of formal and informal information sources*

There are several reasons why managers prefer informal to formal methods of information transfer:

♦ The response and feedback is instant. The whole process is quicker and so is perceived as more efficient (even if the information is only patchy or actually inaccurate).

♦ Being personal, it is targeted at the recipient, so some initial filtering will have been carried out (but is this the half of the picture you want and need...?).

♦ They might not know what useful formal information is available, or how to access it.

♦ Cultural reasons: decisions are often made on the basis of experience and judgement, not painstaking fact finding.

In practice, it makes sense to use a mix of formal and informal, hard and soft data to get a complete picture.

Table 1.2 shows some typical information needs and the information sources that might meet them.

Need/purpose	Types of information	
Produce a report on ice-cream sales for June	Who asked for the report and who will read it Projected and actual sales figures Previous year's figures Meteorological data Report of June launch of new ice-cream product by major competitor	
Your awareness of your own organisational environment (keeping your finger on the pulse)	Company reports and budgets Products and services launched or axed Internal newsletters and memos Meetings	Discussions at the coffee machine Share price Competitor share price
Competitor intelligence	Press reports on company performance and activities Market research data/market analysis Company websites Company annual reports	Trade journals News reports Share price Trends analysis and forecasting Industry gossip

Table 1.2 *Examples of information needs and sources*

Activity 2
Categorise information sources

Objective

Use this activity to analyse the different kinds of information you use on a regular basis.

Task

1 In the first column in the chart provided, note down eight information sources that you use on a regular basis.

2 Categorise them as formal or informal, internal or external, electronic, hard copy or verbal, hard (factual) or soft (impressionistic or qualitative).

3 Score them for usefulness on a scale of 1 to 5, where 1 is low usefulness and 5 is high usefulness.

4 Identify your three most useful sources, and analyse why these are the most useful.

Information source	Formal or informal	Internal or external	Electronic, hard copy or verbal	Hard or soft	Usefulness 1 = low 5 = high
					☐ ☐ ☐ ☐ ☐ 1 2 3 4 5
					☐ ☐ ☐ ☐ ☐ 1 2 3 4 5
					☐ ☐ ☐ ☐ ☐ 1 2 3 4 5
					☐ ☐ ☐ ☐ ☐ 1 2 3 4 5
					☐ ☐ ☐ ☐ ☐ 1 2 3 4 5
					☐ ☐ ☐ ☐ ☐ 1 2 3 4 5
					☐ ☐ ☐ ☐ ☐ 1 2 3 4 5
					☐ ☐ ☐ ☐ ☐ 1 2 3 4 5

Three best sources	Analysis

Feedback

You may have found that you mainly use informal and electronic data, largely because it's accessible, or that you have a definite preference for hard data as it gives you the facts. Build on this activity by considering whether you are making full use of all the sources that might be useful for your purpose. For example, if you tend to use hard data, think about whether seeking opinions may give you different, valuable perspectives. Think about how you can improve the usefulness of the sources, for example, can you be clearer about what you want from the source? See also Theme 2: *Evaluating information.*

Information as an aid to decision making

Much decision making is based on our inbuilt mental models and knowledge base, but this tacit information source can be corroborated and enhanced by formal decision-support mechanisms.

The decision-making process

How do *you* make decisions? Do you assemble all the facts relating to the problem? Rely on your experience and insight? Shut your eyes and hope for the best? Most people do some or all of these things at different times, depending on the nature of the decision. However, the decision-making process shown in Figure 1.4 describes the basic steps involved in consciously making a decision.

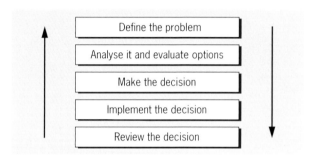

Figure 1.4 *The decision-making process*

The key step is the second one: analyse and evaluate options. Whatever the problem – sorting out a production schedule, conducting a staff appraisal, negotiating a deal – you will need either consciously or unconsciously to weigh up the situation and make decisions accordingly.

An increasing difficulty facing managers now is the speed at which these decisions have to be made: there is just no time for detailed investigation. In an age when managers are faced with more and more information, there is less and less time in which to evaluate its usefulness. As a result, decisions are made on the basis of partial information, wrong information – or whatever information is *available*, rather than *appropriate*.

The concept of cause and effect is commonly used in the way people argue and reason. In making our choices, it is important to identify the right causes and effects – it is all too easy to focus on the symptoms rather than the root causes. It is also necessary to consider your decision-making criteria – what you want to achieve, within what time frame, with what resources. This does assume, of course, that there is a single 'right' decision that you can make to achieve a predictable, successful outcome.

Informix, a software development company, carried out a survey in 1999 to examine how decisions are made in different organisations around the world, and to find out how well the available information, in all its forms, supported the decision-making process. A general finding was that managers, even when they are supported by a multitude of different information sources, find decision making extremely stressful. Most of these managers quoted examples of major decisions that were made incorrectly in the previous six months, and the larger the organisation, the more likely it was to have had a problem.

One of the most important detrimental factors affecting decision making was limited, incorrect or misinterpreted data.

Some key findings of the survey:

♦ 32 per cent of the sample had made an important business decision in the past six months based on hope or luck

♦ the single biggest cause of stress in decision making is a lack of information

♦ 33 per cent of managers ignore relevant data either when making a decision in the first place or when it becomes apparent that a decision has been incorrect.

Source: *Informix* (1999)

What happens when it goes wrong? Below are some examples of information disasters, where the information needed to make decisions was unavailable or ignored:

♦ On 19 October 1987, the Dow Jones Industrial Average took its biggest one-day plunge in the history of the US Stock Market. A major factor in this was that information systems malfunctioned and impeded information flows.

♦ In the same month, British meteorologists failed to appreciate the strength of the oncoming winds which led to one of the biggest storms in living memory: they ignored the available information.

♦ Nuclear scientists at Three Mile Island, and later Chernobyl, failed to take account quickly enough of the information coming from their instrumentation to prevent accidents happening.

Catastrophes of all manner can and do ensue because of what the behavioural scientist might call 'dysfunctional information attitudes and behaviours'. This is a fancy phrase that means that information has been mismanaged somehow, somewhere, by someone, at some time, and often with disastrous consequences in terms of human misery, political misfortune or business failure.

Source: *Horton and Lewis* (1991)

Let's look more closely at the kinds of decision making in which managers are involved.

Levels of management decisions

Management decisions are made at three broad levels within the organisation, and each type of decision has its own characteristics:

Operational decisions: these are the day-to-day decisions affecting the running of the organisation. The decisions tend to be short term (days or weeks) and need to be made quite frequently. For example, a supermarket deciding on whether it needs to order more strawberries to cope with current demand.

Tactical decisions: these have a longer time frame (months or years) and tend to be made by middle managers who are directly involved in implementing the policies of the organisation. For example, a toy shop timing the start of its Christmas promotion.

Strategic decisions: these are made by top management, and since they affect the organisational plans of the whole business, possibly for a number of years, they are not made very frequently. For example, whether to sell off a subsidiary company in response to falling profits.

All these decisions will require information, but the type of information that is needed will be different for each level of decision making. See Figure 1.5.

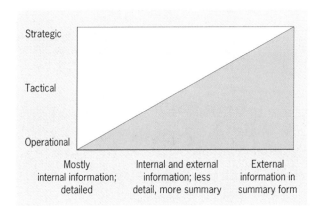

Figure 1.5 *Characteristics of information for management decisions*

Source: *Nickerson* (2001)

Operational decisions rely mostly on internal, detailed data: how many strawberries did we sell yesterday, or last weekend? **Tactical** decisions involve a wider spread of less detailed information: for the past two years, what were the sales figures for the month prior to the Christmas promotion and during the promotion? **Strategic** decisions may use long-term performance figures from inside the organisation, but also financial forecasts and analyses from the wider marketplace, its own shareholders' views, and so on.

Cross-functional, in-house systems such as accounting, finance, marketing and human resources (HR) can, of course, support decision making at every level of the organisation, whether operational, tactical or strategic. There are also general *types* of information systems for management support, which we will look at a little later in this section.

Getting the right information to make decisions

In an ideal world, getting the right information to make decisions would be very easy. We would just type a question into our PC, or know exactly the right person we need to telephone in order to get an instant, accurate and authoritative answer.

In real life, most of us have to get by without perfect one-stop solutions. Where do we get the information we need to make decisions when our systems are not organisation wide, but are locked into 'silos' where we can perhaps drill down to increasing levels of detail, but not across to the vital missing piece of data that is held within another department?

If you think of a decision you have made recently and about where the information came from, you will probably realise that it is a mix of your own knowledge, whatever information was available and maybe a chat to a couple of colleagues who always seem to have an answer or know where to find one. Think a little more broadly: how does your team get the information it needs in order to operate? The model would probably look something like the one shown in Figure 1.6.

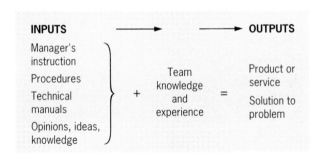

Figure 1.6 *Information for team operations*

In this model, the inputs (your basic raw materials) come from a diverse mix of sources. Some of these will be formal, some very informal – but no less valuable for that. These inputs will be processed by individuals or the team to produce the desired outputs (a specific product or service, or the solution to a problem). Getting it right assumes that the flow of information, both formal and informal, is:

◆ unimpeded – there are no bottlenecks and blockages (human or technical)

◆ able to move upwards, downwards and sideways with equal ease

◆ equally accessible to all who need it.

An organisational approach to take some of the luck out of getting the right information for decision making – for making individual knowledge explicit and sharing it across the organisation – is to develop formal information systems to support managers.

Formal information systems for management support

Computer systems that can store and manipulate information provide a structured and accessible support for management decision making. Here are descriptions of three kinds of systems in common use: management information systems (MIS), decision support systems (DSS) and executive support systems (ESS).

Management information systems (MIS)

A management information system, or MIS, supports management decisions by providing information in the form of reports and responses to queries to managers at different levels within an organisation. The MIS database that provides the information to the manager comes from both inside and outside the organisation, much of it from the data stored in transaction processing systems – the nuts and bolts of day-to-day operations and processes.

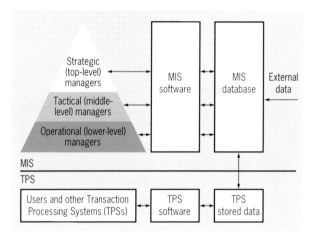

Figure 1.7 *Structure of an MIS*   Source: *Nickerson* (2001)

Decision support systems (DSS)

Whereas an MIS provides information from a database with little or no analysis, a decision support system (DSS) helps managers by analysing data from a database and providing them with the results, often in the form of statistical calculations or mathematical models. It is used most often for decisions at tactical and strategic levels. The main system components are the DSS database that contains the data, and the model base which contains the mathematical models and statistical calculation routines that are used to analyse data from the database. Decision support systems are often used in situations where decisions are unstructured or semi-structured, and are good for working through 'what if' scenarios to calculate the effects of different decisions on outcomes (what happens if we start the Christmas promotion two weeks earlier?)

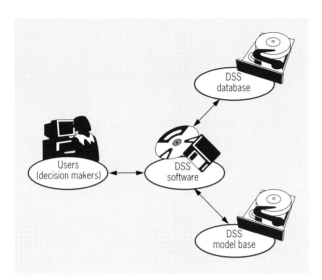

Figure 1.8 *Structure of a DSS*   Source: *Nickerson* (2001)

A variation on this is a group DSS, typically used in a networked environment where several PCs are joined together, in which users can collaborate to reach a group decision.

Executive support systems (ESS)

Also known as executive information systems, these are designed to support strategic business decisions. Although strategic decisions usually involve summarised information, there is often a need for a specific level of detail to pinpoint a particular problem. For example, executives in an organisation that is thinking of selling off a failing subsidiary might want to try to discover where its failure lies: is it a particular market segment, a region, a product line? This will often require a drilling-down process to get from general information to highly specific data subsets.

The user of an ESS will typically need to access a wide variety of databases: internal, external, those created by the individual user and electronic mailboxes.

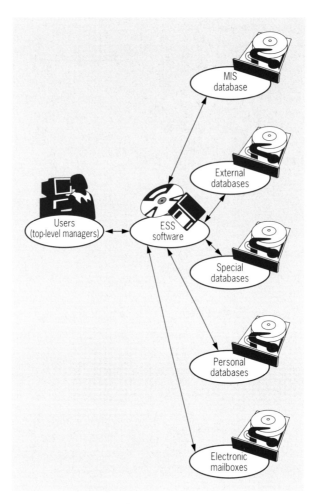

Figure 1.9 *Structure of an ESS*   Source: *Nickerson* (2001)

Other systems

Increasingly, managers are looking at more sophisticated methods such as **expert systems** that mimic the way a human would analyse a situation and recommend a particular course of action, and **knowledge management systems** that can organise, store and enable shared access to the collective knowledge of the organisation.

The point to remember about all of these systems is that the quality of the output is only as good as the quality of the input.

The activities that follow explore the theme of information flows and systems for management support. You will start by looking at your information sources.

Activity 3
Explore information for decision making

Objective

Use this activity to assess whether you have the appropriate information you need to make decisions.

Task

1　Think of a decision you need to make in your work at the moment or in the near future. Write this at the top of the table provided.

2　What information do you believe is essential for you to make a well-informed decision? List the information in the first column.

3　In the second column, note down where you think you can find this information – who has this information, what form is it in?

4　In the final column, assess whether you can get access to each piece of information to help you to make your decision. If it is available, is it in a form that you can use?

5　What are the implications of the availability of the information on the quality of your decision?

Decision:		
Information required	Source?	Can you access it?

Implications for quality of the decision:

Feedback

Managers rarely have access to all the information they need to make good decisions. You may well have found that the right kind of information is available, but not when you need it or in a form that you can use. However, the decisions still have to be made, in spite of gaps in the information or contradictory information.

You have to bring your judgement and experience to bear when making a decision based on incomplete information. You often have to make assumptions based on an unclear situation. Be aware of any limitations in the information used to make a decision so that you know how 'safe' the decision is likely to be. By doing this, you can take corrective action quickly if new information comes to light.

You may find Theme 2 on information overload and evaluating information helpful in improving your use of information for decision making.

Activity 4
Plot information flows within your team

Objective

This activity will help you to identify the way information flows around your team.

Task

1 Select a key process or activity carried out by team members. It could be one that you or your team believes is not working very well.

2 Answer the following questions about the activity and record your responses in the chart provided.

   ◆ What are the main steps involved in this activity? (Note the decisions, actions or outputs.)

   ◆ Who is involved at each step? (List the team members who carry out each step and who need to be kept informed at each step.)

   ◆ What information is needed to carry out each step? (There may be a need for several items of information in different forms.)

   ◆ Where does this information come from? (It may come from a customer, from someone else within the team or from another part of the organisation.)

   ◆ Who receives this information? (List the person or people who receive the information.)

♦ What does that person do with the information? (For example store it, use it to carry out the step, pass it on to another person, use it for another purpose unrelated to the step.)

3 Now review your responses. You may want to do this with your team. Do team members have the information they need for each step? Does the information go to the right people?

Process/activity: Steps	*Who is involved*	*Info needed*	*Source*	*Who receives*	*Action taken*

Feedback

This activity may have given you some insights into the way information flows around your unit/department for one particular process/activity. In an ideal world, the flow of information would be clearly related to its purpose. However, you may have identified practices such as information short cuts (which bypass people who need to know), toing and froing of requests or problems, or a heavy concentration of a small number of key people who are involved in information transactions whether they need to be or not. Use the activity to clarify information needs and regularise gaps or other deficiencies.

Activity 5
Specify an information system for management support

Objective

Use this activity to clarify the kind of decision support that you would like to see from an information system.

Task

Assume that you can specify and purchase an information system to help you in your job.

1 Think about the features you would like an information system to have in order to give you the most benefit in terms of making it easier for you to do your job to a high standard. In the chart provided, note these features and the benefits they would bring.

2 In the third column, tick the features/benefits that are already available to support you in your current information system.

Features	Benefits – how each feature would help you do your work	Already available?
		☐
		☐
		☐
		☐
		☐

3 Now think about which of the following types of information system would best be able to give you the features you require.

- ◆ Management information system?
- ◆ Decision support system?
- ◆ Executive support system?

Which system will best provide the required features, and why?

Feedback

Working on this activity should highlight any weaknesses in your existing support structure or the need for a more sophisticated information system. Consult with colleagues in your IT department to see whether any of your identified improvements can be implemented.

Using the Web as an information resource

Here we provide some very practical guidance on finding the information you need, both to make informed decisions and to build up your own knowledge base in your chosen area. It will not eliminate all the problems involved in finding Web-based material, but should give you some sharper tools to help you along the way.

Search engines

Note that although the World Wide Web is technically only a part of the Internet, it is the one that is most familiar to most people, and the terms 'Web' and 'Internet' are used interchangeably.

The starting point for all Web searches is a **search engine** – quite literally, a force that responds to an information request by searching the Web for what it interprets as relevant material. Search engines are also referred to here as **indexes** as they act like gigantic indexes to selected chunks of the Web. They take an input search word (**search term**) or phrase, and retrieve a set of results (**hits**) that relate to that term or phrase from the Web pages that they have identified, collected into a virtual database and indexed. Note the word 'selected' – none of them scans absolutely everything, and you will need to learn which search engines are most useful for which purposes.

There are four basic types of search tool:

◆ free text search engines
◆ human-generated indexes
◆ metasearch tools
◆ natural language tools.

As search engines develop, the distinction between the types is becoming more blurred.

Free text search engines

Search engines retrieve a set of Web pages (hits) that match a word or phrase input by the user. They do not search the entire Web – only those pages that exist in the index of the search engine. The indexes are compiled by computer robots and can be vast. Google (www.google.com) and Alta Vista (www.altavista.com) are currently the biggest with billions of pages each. Since the indexing method is basically a free text search, the engine will retrieve every instance of the search term, whether it is relevant to your search or not. This means that if you're a bird enthusiast looking for information on 'cranes', you will also retrieve references to heavy lifting gear, maybe crane flies and companies that have crane in their title. On the other hand, these searches may not pick up useful **related terms**, so a search on 'boats' may not select references to 'yachts' or 'ships'. This is an area that is improving all the time.

Index based search engines

Some companies also try to catalogue the Web. Whereas search engines use computers to create the search engine index, classified and specialist directories use humans to select and catalogue the Web pages. Yahoo (www.yahoo.com) is one of the most notable. As well as being able to enter search text, the user can also browse through the directory. For example, if you want to find a new movie, you might start with entertainment and then click movies and carry on until you find what you want.

There are numerous specialist directories that act as gateways to specific subjects on the Web. The medical gateway www.omni.ac.uk is an example. For a comprehensive list of what is available, go to www.vlib.org.

Metasearch engines

These are not search engines themselves – more tools that know about other search tools and will submit your query to several search engines at once. Metacrawler (www.metacrawler.com) and Dogpile (www.dogpile.com) are examples.

Natural language search engines

Natural language search engines are very appealing, as you can literally type in a question in the way that you would ask it. Ask Jeeves is probably the best known of these. Inputting: 'Who won the World Cup in 1998?' retrieves not only the result but details of many other World Cup and football-related sites.

Table 1.3 summarises the main types of search engines and what they are most useful for.

Type of search engine	Example	What it's most useful for
Free text search engines	Google	When you know exactly what you want and can be specific about it. Good for 'Mercedes-Benz'; bad for 'performance cars'
Index-based search engines	Yahoo	An overview of the subject area, structured so that you can narrow down a search or make it broader. For example, from 'astrophotography' you can go up to the broader category 'astronomy' or down to the more specific 'lunar eclipse photography'
Metasearch engines	Dogpile	A broad and comprehensive view of sites in a subject area
Natural language search	Ask Jeeves	Good for novice searchers, or if you want a general look around a subject area
Specialist indexes	Omni	In-depth access to a highly specific subject area

Table 1.3 *Main types of search engines*

A list of selected search engines is provided at the end of this section.

Getting better results

Choosing the right kind of search engine for your purpose will go a long way towards getting better search results more quickly. There are a couple of other things you can do too.

Advanced search

One of these is to take advantage of any advanced search facilities offered by the search engines. These should make your search more specific, and more likely to retrieve focused results rather than irrelevant hits (**false drops**).

For some search engines, such as Excite, HotBot and Lycos, this kind of search supports the use of **Boolean operators**. These sound alarming but are really quite simple, and consist of just three words which you can incorporate into your search phrase: AND, OR and NOT.

You may have noticed AND appearing in the search header when you are running a search. What it means is that only items that have all elements of the search phrase in them will be retrieved. For example, 'bottling AND canning' will only produce results where *both* the terms 'bottling' and 'canning' appear in the same item.

OR will find all occurrences of the terms in your search phrase whether they are together or not. So 'bottling OR canning' will retrieve all items containing 'bottling', all items containing 'canning' and all items containing both terms. You will see from this that the effect of OR is to *broaden* your search, leading to a greater number of hits.

NOT is used to narrow a search. In our example, 'bottling NOT canning' will retrieve items which relate to 'bottling' but will exclude those which contain a reference to 'canning'.

In search engines such as Google and Yahoo, the Boolean operators have been replaced by signs such as '+' and '–' for words to include or exclude. Some searches can also be restricted by date or other criteria such as language, or expanded by the use of 'wildcard' characters. Search results will also be affected by whether you input a phrase in quotes or not (try 'London Bridge' and London Bridge). Check out any help notes and search tips offered by a search engine from an advanced search facility to make the most of your time online. They do vary – compare the advanced search facilities offered by Google or Yahoo and Alta Vista.

Don't forget you can also search for images, audio and video – Google claims to offer the most comprehensive resource of images, with 250 million of them.

Bookmarking

Finding the information once is one thing; finding it a second time is another. Make full use of your bookmarking facility to set up topic folders that you can refer to later and update periodically.

Some tips for effective use of the Internet

- Be prepared to put in some time at first to surf around and get a good idea of the main websites in your area of interest

- Try out different search engines to see how the results compare

- Set up folders of bookmarked sites to create your own virtual library – but check the URLs (uniform resource locator, the address of a Web page) from time to time to see if they're still valid

- Take advantage of any online help or advanced search tips offered by the search engines.

You will also find useful advice on Internet searching on the sites of experts such as Phil Bradley (www.philb.com) and Karen Blakeman (www.rba.co.uk) or check out Manchester Metropolitan University at www.hlss.mmu.ac.uk/dic/main/howto.html

Keeping up to date

Another important aspect of quality information for decision making is that the information needs to be up to date.

One way of doing this is by joining mailing lists and newsgroups in your area of interest. A good place to start is http://groups.google.com which offers a list of groups to browse in all subject areas.

For the latest news and current affairs, there is a huge selection on offer. All the major search engines will have a news service of some kind (try looking at Yahoo or Northern Light) though some will have a strong US bias. As you might expect, the BBC is an excellent source of business news (www.bbc.co.uk/1/hi/business/default.stm) and the Financial Times is a popular site (www.ft.com). A more personalised offering is Create Your Own Newspaper or CRAYON, which allows you to personalise your own information sources and subject areas (for details see www.crayon.net/using/how.html).

The last few years have seen the rise of robots (**bots**) or **intelligent agents**, which can 'learn' your requirements and scurry around the Web looking for information on your behalf. They are more effective than average search tools for two reasons (Edmunds and Morris, 2000):

◆ An intelligent agent can make decisions on the basis of the data it acquires without needing direct instruction from the user

◆ Because it is able to learn about individual preferences, it can predict the likelihood of items it comes across being of interest.

For information on these clever little creatures, go to BotSpot (www.botspot.com) which describes hundreds of them (start with What's a Bot? or the FAQs section). The site includes a list of bots by category. These include several Update bots which can monitor your favourite websites and report on new developments.

Selected search engines:
◆ Google (www.google.com)
◆ Alta Vista (www.altavista.com)
◆ Ask Jeeves (www.ask.com)
◆ Dogpile (www.dogpile.com)
◆ Excite (www.excite.com)
◆ HotBot (www.hotbot.com)
◆ Lycos (www.lycos.com)
◆ Metacrawler (www.metacrawler.com)
◆ Northern Light (www.northernlight.com)
◆ Yahoo! (www.yahoo.com)

If you're looking for non-English language search engines, try Searchengine Colossus (www.searchenginecolossus.com) which covers about 100 countries.

Activity 6
Use the Web for research

Objectives

If you are not experienced in using the Web for research, use this activity to:

♦ practise using the Web to find the information you need

♦ consider how far the Web can help you to carry out aspects of your job.

Task

1   You are going to Paris this coming weekend. Use the Web to find out:

♦ whether you will need to take an umbrella with you (the answer is not that you will buy an umbrella when you get there)

♦ the current rate of exchange.

Keep a note of how long it takes you to find this information.

2   How do you think the Web will help in your work and in your development programme? Write your thoughts below.

How the Web will help in my work and development programme:

Feedback

1 How successful you were, and how quickly you found the information, will partly depend on which search engine you began with. Finding a five-day weather forecast is fairly straightforward, but you might have had to work a bit harder to get at the exchange rate.

2 Your response here is likely to depend on the nature of your work, and how successfully you are currently using the Web to find information. Some people find the Web frustrating and slow to use at first. The quality of websites can also cause problems if they are not user-friendly.

Although the following is not a comprehensive list, if you need to do any of these activities as part of your work, you should find the Web helpful:

◆ Track and keep up to date with news events – including business news and share prices

◆ Find out government trends or statistics

◆ Get government guidelines on matters affecting business, for example employment law, the introduction of the euro, quality in business

◆ Find out about management theory, models and techniques

◆ Find bibliographic information

◆ Check out competitor information

◆ Research supplier companies

◆ Find new employees

◆ Find out what non-governmental organisations are doing.

Some organisations also use the Internet for business-to-business commerce. It becomes a marketplace.

Find out whether your organisation has a policy about using the Internet at work for research. Some organisations, concerned about inappropriate access to the Web at work, restrict or monitor its use.

◆ Recap

Consider the differences between data, information and knowledge

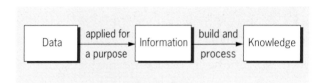

◆ Information may be:

- electronic, hard copy or verbal
- quantitative or qualitative.

Identify and evaluate the sources of information that you use

◆ Information sources may be:

- Internal or external
- Formal or informal.

◆ Managers often prefer informal sources because the data is instantly available, but using a mix of hard and soft information from formal and informal sources is a more reliable foundation for decision making. As a manager, you need to cultivate a range of information sources to meet your needs.

◆ The information you need depends to a large extent on the types of decisions you make. Operational decisions can be made on the basis of internal data whereas strategic decisions require data and analyses from external sources.

Assess whether information flows effectively within your team and identify areas for improvement

◆ Analysing the flow of information into your team may reveal blockages or bottlenecks, or that some people cannot access the information they need. This provides a basis for improving operational processes and decision making.

◆ Computer systems are used to improve the flow of information. The different levels of decision making are supported by three types of system: management information systems, decision support systems and executive support systems.

Analyse how effectively you use the Internet as an information source

◆ The four main types of search tool are: free text search engines, human-generated indexes, metasearch tools and natural language search enagines.

◆ Choosing the right search engine and developing your knowledge of advanced search techniques will increase your efficiency and improve your search results.

 ## More @

Wilson, D. (2002) *Managing Information: IT for Business Process*, **Butterworth-Heinemann**
This book describes how successful organisations make best use of information and knowledge and explains why information technology is essential for the management of business processes.

Argyris, C. (1999) *On Organisational Learning*, **Blackwell Publishers**
This book for managers and development specialists provides more on double loop learning and how organisations evolve and learn. Try also www.infed.org/thinkers/argyris.htm for an overview of Argyris's work.

Buckley, P. and Clark, D. (2004) *A Rough Guide to the Internet*, **Rough guides**
Written in plain English, this book covers everything from getting online for the first time to advanced tips and tricks.

Information Week at www.informationweek.com and **BetterManagement** at www.bettermanagement.com are both useful sites to search for downloadable articles, white papers and research reports.

2 Evaluating information

A constant flow of information is essential for all of us to run our lives and businesses, but what happens when we get too much of it? The concept of information overload isn't new – indeed it goes back centuries – but the huge expansion in publishing in the 19th century, and radio and TV in the early part of the 20th century, was already causing noticeable problems by the late 1950s. Now, with even greater growth of electronic information, individuals and organisations need to devise a whole new set of strategies to deal with the massive volumes of information that we all encounter day after day.

This will involve the ability to evaluate our information sources so that we can instantly discard what is irrelevant. It will also require us to consider more carefully the information we give out to other people – and the number of people we give it to. Refining the concept of fitness for purpose – the right information at the right time – and making this available across a shared-access system can help to improve the way in which we manage the growing volume of information.

In this theme you will:

◆ **Identify information overload and assess why it occurs**

◆ **Evaluate the information you receive by assessing its quality and value to you**

◆ **Reduce your information overload.**

Information overload

Are you subjected to 'infoglut' or 'data smog'? Is it giving you 'analysis paralysis'? The literature on information overload has invented some striking terms for a condition that many people claim to suffer from.

But what is information overload? Here is one definition:

> Information overload occurs when information received becomes a hindrance rather than a help, when the information is potentially useful...

Source: *Bawden et al.* (1999)

Common feelings associated with information overload are that you feel overwhelmed, in a situation that's out of your control and faced with more information than anyone can possibly handle. You don't know which of the many pieces of information are the important ones, or indeed whether there are more pieces of information still to come before you can make an intelligent decision. The resulting feelings of helplessness can have a major impact on the health of employees and their efficiency and effectiveness within organisations.

A survey carried out by Reuters in 1996 revealed that:

♦ two-thirds of managers surveyed believed that information overload not only caused a loss of job satisfaction but also affected their personal relationships

♦ half thought it had damaged their health

♦ nearly half believed that important decisions were delayed and affected by having too much information.

Source: *Reuters* (1996)

How does it happen?

There are various reasons why managers collect more information than they can handle:

♦ There's a lot more information around to collect, and it's increasing all the time

♦ A general increase in unsolicited information (think of all the junk mail you get)

♦ The fear of missing out on some vital piece of information that your colleagues may already know about

♦ The perception that this is what you have to do to be well informed

♦ To justify the decisions you make

♦ To collect information in case it might be useful one day

♦ Having a piled up in-tray and a cluttered desk demonstrates how busy and important you are

♦ You get the same information from a lot of different sources (this includes reports and articles which basically repeat a large percentage of their content)

♦ Cross-checking that the original information you have is accurate

♦ Getting on everyone's 'copy-to' (cc) mail list so that you don't miss out

♦ Poor information searching skills, so that a lot of irrelevant information is retrieved.

Research published shows that companies risk wasting their investment in technology implemented to manage information because they are failing to tackle the 'human hurdle' – up to two thirds of respondents had problems with information overload, employees not having time to share knowledge and reinventing the wheel.

Source: *Information Management Report* (2000)

So, we're getting more information, more rapidly, from more sources, in more formats – and less and less time to deal with it.

Activity 7
Assess the extent of your information overload

Objective

Use this activity to assess how far you are overloading yourself with unnecessary information.

Task

Fill in the following questionnaire by ticking all the statements that apply to you.

I often collect more information than I need in case I miss out on something vital	☐
I need to gather a lot of information to keep myself well informed	☐
I need a lot of information to justify the decisions I make	☐
I often collect information in case it might come in handy in the future	☐
I have to get on lots of people's 'cc' lists so that I know what's going on	☐
I have to collect a lot of information so that I can cross-check its validity	☐
I find that my searches for information often produce a lot of irrelevant data	☐

Feedback

There are no 'right' answers, but your work on this activity might have given you pause for thought. You may like to consider:

♦ Are there other, better ways of keeping up to date?

♦ Can I improve my searching and information retrieval skills?

♦ Should I be more confident in my decision making?

Evaluating information

For our decision making to be quality decision making, the information that supports it needs to be quality information. But what does 'quality' actually mean in this context? How can we recognise and measure it? What criteria or benchmarks can we use? One difficulty is that, over time, the quantitative and qualitative value of information can decay. Also, information quality in this context can be considered from the point of view of function (does it do what it is meant to do and what are the functions it satisfies or supports?) or of form (the image or intangible benefits that accrue from having the information).

What's the added value?

For some experts, the problem of information overload is to a great extent part of a failure to create 'quality' information – that is, information that has real value-added content. This of course assumes that you have a very clear idea of what it is that makes a piece of information add value.

Simpson and Prusak (1995) believe that the value of information can only be measured in terms of the benefit you get from using it. But how do you measure this 'benefit in use'? Many approaches have been tried but none has stood the test of real-time business practice, and yet individuals try to add value in their own communications all the time! Think back to your last couple of conversations. Were any of the people involved:

◆ trying to verify the information given ('Well, you say that, but is it actually true?')

◆ drawing conclusions from the information ('It looks as if what we've got here is...')

◆ challenging something that didn't sound quite right ('Hang on a minute...that can't be right...')?

During these kinds of conversations, although you may not be aware of it, you are evaluating the information you received so that you can work out what to do about it.

From this kind of instinctive evaluation, Simpson and Prusak have devised a model that proposes five universal elements of value in information, shown in Figure 2.1.

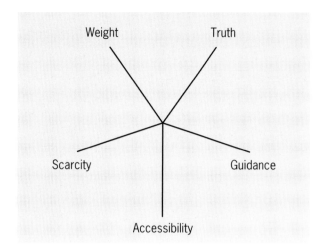

Figure 2.1 *Adding value to information*

Source: *Adapted from Simpson and Prusak* (1995)

Let's look at each of the five universal elements.

Truth. How confident are you about the validity of the information? In operational or systems terms, its validity or otherwise may be obvious; in management processes, where you are dealing with a mix of factual information, inferences and subjective judgement, things may be less clear-cut. But you will still need to have a high degree of confidence in the information if you are to make a decision based on it.

Scarcity. This refers to the value of information which is 'new' or not freely available to competitor organisations. There may be little that is new at first glance in your day-to-day operating data. However, using freely available information combined in a new way, or with a flash of insight, can produce something that provides your organisation with a real advantage over the competition.

Guidance. This is the extent to which information points the way to what action needs to be taken in a certain situation or set of circumstances. This is most obvious in sets of procedures or instructions, but information can also give guidance where you are highlighting a problem or diagnosing the causes of a problem.

Accessibility. This is the availability of information to its potential users when it is needed and in a form that they can use. Information is only of use if people know about it, can get at it and can understand it. An important element of this is the way the information is presented – does it encourage and help understanding by the user?

Weight. This is what prompts recipients to treat the information so seriously that they will act on it. It will incorporate things like relevance to the user's situation, timeliness and accuracy. It sometimes has very little to do with the information itself, but is closely tied up with the credibility or authority of the person providing the information.

Evaluating information from the Internet

These five universal elements can be applied to information generated within or outside the organisation. They can be used to evaluate information received over the Internet. You can use the following checklist to evaluate sites that are dedicated to a particular organisation or based around a specific subject area. Each question is followed by the most relevant universal element of evaluation:

Checklist for evaluating websites

- Is the purpose of the site clear? (Guidance)

- Are contact details and basic information easy to find? (Accessibility)

- Is the coverage of the site appropriate for its purpose? (Accessibility)

- Does the institution responsible for the site have an established reputation and expertise? (Weight)

- Is the information likely to be accurate? (Truth)

- Is the information current? Are there details of when it was last updated? (Weight)

- Is a site map provided? Is navigation clear and straightforward? (Guidance)

- Is the information well presented and arranged? (Accessibility)

- Does the site compare well with those of similar organisations or those in the same subject area? (Weight)

- Are there good help facilities? (Guidance)

- Does the site provide links to other sites, or supporting materials? (Guidance)

- Are these other sites or supporting materials useful? (Truth)

Source: *Based on Cooke* (1999)

Activity 8
Evaluate your incoming information

Objective

Use this activity to evaluate the usefulness of the information you receive in your day-to-day job.

Task

1 In the chart provided, log all the mail (internal, external and e-mail) that you receive in the course of one day.

2 Give each item a score (1 = low and 5 = high) for the universal elements of:

   ♦ **truth** (your level of confidence in the validity of the information)

   ♦ **scarcity** (new information or providing new insights)

   ♦ **guidance** (points the way to action or the diagnosis of a problem)

   ♦ **accessibility** (availability of information when it is needed and in a form in which you can understand it)

   ♦ **weight** (relevance or the authority of the sender).

3 From your scores you should be able to see how much of this is 'quality' information and fit for your present purpose.

4 Discuss your findings with colleagues.

Mail item	Truth 1–5	Scarcity 1–5	Guidance 1–5	Accessibility 1–5	Weight 1–5

Mail item	Truth 1–5	Scarcity 1–5	Guidance 1–5	Accessibility 1–5	Weight 1–5

Feedback

Your work on this activity should have given you some ideas about the kinds of information (or informant) that are more (or less) useful to you. Use it to become more selective in your filtering of incoming information.

You should also consider ways to communicate your information needs to those sources that are less than satisfactory. It is possible that small changes can be made that cost very little but make a major difference to the value of that information to you.

Activity 9
Evaluating websites

Objective

Use this activity to explore websites and evaluate their effectiveness.

Task

Evaluate the following websites by rating them from 1 to 5 against each item in the checklist provided. Circle 1 to denote very poor quality; circle 5 to denote very high quality.

BBC – www.bbc.co.uk

McDonald's – www.mcdonalds.com

Singapore Airlines – www.singaporeair.com

	BBC	McDonald's	Singapore Airlines
Purpose of site clear?	1 2 3 4 5	1 2 3 4 5	1 2 3 4 5
Contact details and basic information easy to find?	1 2 3 4 5	1 2 3 4 5	1 2 3 4 5
Coverage appropriate for purpose?	1 2 3 4 5	1 2 3 4 5	1 2 3 4 5
Does the organisation have an established reputation and weight?	1 2 3 4 5	1 2 3 4 5	1 2 3 4 5
Is information likely to be accurate?	1 2 3 4 5	1 2 3 4 5	1 2 3 4 5
Is information current?	1 2 3 4 5	1 2 3 4 5	1 2 3 4 5
Is a site map provided, or is the site easy to navigate?	1 2 3 4 5	1 2 3 4 5	1 2 3 4 5
Is information well presented and arranged?	1 2 3 4 5	1 2 3 4 5	1 2 3 4 5
Does the site compare well with similar organisations?	1 2 3 4 5	1 2 3 4 5	1 2 3 4 5
Are there good help facilities?	1 2 3 4 5	1 2 3 4 5	1 2 3 4 5
Are there links to other sites or supporting materials?	1 2 3 4 5	1 2 3 4 5	1 2 3 4 5
Are these links or supporting materials useful?	1 2 3 4 5	1 2 3 4 5	1 2 3 4 5

Feedback

Discuss your findings with colleagues. Do you share the same general conclusions? Are there any other aspects that you want to evaluate?

Good practice for reducing overload

There is no single tool or technique that will provide a magic answer to all your information overload problems, but there are techniques that can help. Bawden et al. (1999) divide these techniques into **managerial** and **technical**.

Managerial techniques

On the managerial side, a lot of the techniques come under the general heading of time management. You can re-take control of your information by managing your time more effectively, using some of the following techniques:

- Structure your information searching more intelligently, and link it directly to your goal: why are you looking for this information, and how can you best find it? This is likely to be quicker and more effective than just surfing in a random way, hoping that something useful will turn up.

- Follow the classic time-management recommendation and 'handle a piece of paper only once' (the same applies to electronic messages). Take action on it immediately or delete/bin it.

- Be very selective about the newsgroups and mailing lists you join – they can generate a lot of irrelevant information that is time-consuming to read through.

- Delete irrelevant e-mails without reading them.

- Only file material when you know it will be difficult to find it again.

- Improve your own information literacy – your ability to retrieve, evaluate, organise and use information from a variety of sources. This will include effective management of both paper files and e-mail folders.

All this lies within your own hands. If you are looking at reducing organisation-wide information overload, putting out some sensible rules for e-mail etiquette is a good start. The European Forum for Electronic Business has developed a code of practice to help organisations use e-mail more effectively. Here are some of its main points:

Guidelines for using e-mail
- Do you need to e-mail at all? Sometimes it's quicker to telephone.

- Give your messages a meaningful title – not 'Meeting' but 'Team meeting 29 April'.

♦ For clarity (and to save other people's time) restrict action requests to one recipient only, and copy to (cc) anyone else who needs to know.

♦ Keep your messages brief.

♦ Don't mail or cc more people that absolutely necessary.

♦ Think very carefully before putting a message on a distribution list for general use.

♦ Using the 'BCC' (Blanket Carbon Copy) field instead of 'To' for messages to several people will reduce message size.

♦ Currency symbols can be changed in transmission. If your e-mails are likely to contain references to different currencies, it's better to use an agreed alpha abbreviation like GBP for sterling and USD for US dollars.

♦ Use the 'Urgent' flag sparingly, or its impact will be lost.

Source: *Adapted from the European Forum for Electronic Business* (www)

Technical techniques

On the technical side, there are systems for ranking and filtering e-mail and other messages; check for details with your information technology (IT) department. As an individual trying to reduce overload on the Internet, your best approach, as indicated earlier, is to make as much use as you can of personal software agents and any customisation offered by the major search engines.

Activity 10
Use e-mail more effectively

Objective

Use this activity to make more effective use of e-mail.

Task

1 Look at the last 10 e-mails that you received that initiated a dialogue or action (that is, not just responses to e-mails of yours).

2 In the chart provided, note down the message header and sender's initials of one of these e-mails. Then evaluate using the following questions:

◆ Was it necessary to send this e-mail? (Did you need it? Would a telephone call have been quicker?)

◆ Is there a meaningful title so you can find it or file it easily? (For example, not 'meeting' but 'Team meeting on 24 Oct'.)

◆ Was the message sent only to people who need to take action or respond, and were other people copied in ('cc') on a need-to-know basis?

◆ Is the message brief and to the point?

◆ Is required action clear?

3   Use the chart below to note down whether each of the messages meets the above e-etiquette guidelines. Write yes, no, or a short comment in each column.

Message header	Sender's initials	E-mail necessary?	Meaningful header?	Appropriate recipients?	Brief and to the point?	Is required action clear?

4   Review your own e-etiquette by using the same criteria. Note down any areas for improvement.

Ways of improving your e-mails:

Feedback

Discuss your work on this activity with colleagues. You may find it helpful to discuss strategies both to deal with a large volume of incoming e-mails and to increase the effectiveness of the ones you send. Would a good-practice checklist for use within the organisation be a good idea?

◆ Recap

Identify information overload and assess why it occurs

◆ When the amount of information received exceeds that desired or needed by a user, it becomes a hindrance and a potential cause of stress, and the user experiences information overload.

◆ Assessing the extent to which you contribute towards your own information overload is a good first step in improving the way you manage and use information.

Evaluate the information you receive by assessing its quality and value to you

◆ Simpson and Prusak (1995) propose that you can evaluate the quality of information available to you using five criteria: **weight** or importance, **truth** or validity, the extent to which you rely on the information for **guidance**, **accessibility** and **scarcity.**

◆ If you are receiving information that is of poor quality, then communicate your needs to your information source to see whether it can be improved.

Reduce your information overload

◆ You can reduce information overload by becoming more selective about the information – including e-mails – that you access and read, and by developing systems for effectively managing hard and soft information.

▶▶ **More @**

Simpson, C. W. and Prusak, L. (1995), 'Troubles with information overload', *International Journal of Information Management*, Vol. 15, No. 6, 413–425
This is the source article with further information on the Simpson and Prusak model.

Try **Mind Tools** at www.mindtools.com for more on information skills and time management techniques.

Communicating information

People handle astonishing quantities of written text on a daily basis, both consciously and unconsciously: newspapers at breakfast, advertising hoardings and shop fronts on the way to work, reports, memos and e-mail on the desktop. They may read a book on the train home, or pick up a few text messages from friends. It is worth pausing for a moment to think about the different ways in which such channels of communication get their message across to you – and what influences how receptive you are to what they are trying to tell you or persuade you to do. How often do you stop reading – simply switch off your attention – from something that is long-winded, difficult to follow, boring or full of errors?

There are lots of very practical reasons why everyone should aim to communicate clearly:

♦ It makes it easier for the recipient to understand the message, which saves time

♦ Written instructions that are clear and unambiguous are easy to follow and act upon

♦ A good written case can be a powerful aid to influencing

♦ In the case of a dispute (for example a disciplinary case) your written reports may be produced as evidence in an employment tribunal or a court of law

♦ What you record now may be a precedent that will need to be referred to for guidance in the future

♦ If the messages aren't understood by the reader, do they count as communication or just a waste of your time and everyone else's?

Many successful business leaders have recognised that the ability to write persuasively – getting people to take their message on board or do what they want them to do – is a key skill. The most effective documents, whether long or short, are those where the author has taken the trouble to ensure maximum impact.

In this theme you will:

♦ **Identify the features of clear written communication**

♦ **Evaluate your writing style**

♦ **Plan an effective presentation**

♦ **Develop notes and visual aids to support your presentation.**

Planning and structuring your document

You may think that a logical approach is the best way to do this. Surely the facts will speak for themselves? Or perhaps you think that if you really want to get your own way quickly, a bit of coercion will do the trick? Andrew Leigh (1997) believes that learning to develop a persuasive writing style is the best way of encouraging people to accept and endorse what you have to say.

Purpose

An important aspect of this is the purpose of the document, which you need to be absolutely clear about:

- What do you want your readers to do?
- What outcome do you want to achieve?

Readers

An essential step in planning a document is to put yourself in the reader's shoes, and to try to predict how they will understand and react to it. Consider the following questions:

- What do your readers expect to gain by reading your document?
- What length of document will be appropriate for the purpose and the recipient? Are they likely to want a one-page summary or a 10-page analysis?
- How much time will they have to read it?
- What is their likely standpoint on the topic, and how can you counter resistance?
- What questions are they likely to raise?

Since your aim is to communicate with people and persuade them rather than to antagonise them at the outset, it is always useful to start by establishing some common ground and getting across that you understand and respect their position. This is important, even if you then go on to provide evidence that their position is no longer tenable and that they will have to consider changing it.

Structure

You can strengthen whatever case you are making (and this applies to the shortest e-mail or longest report) if you structure a document carefully so that:

- the information in it is prioritised, with the most important information coming first – this will mean giving the 'headlines' and main conclusions first, not leaving the punchline until the end

- you have carefully selected what to include and what to omit – this involves thinking about what information your readers need

- you give some indication of what should or will happen next – in other words your recommendations.

Politeness and clarity will get you a long way. However, there are other means of ensuring that your message is received positively, such as style and tone.

Style and tone

You may not have much leeway with style, as a corporate house style may exist that you have to adhere to. If you are not restricted by a corporate house style, you can make your style more interesting by using active language rather than passive.

Think about the difference between:

- 'It is generally recognised within the company that ...' and

- 'As you know...'

Or the difference between:

- 'The project outline was put together by the author of this document' and

- 'I put the project outline together'.

Keep the language simple and straightforward by avoiding features such as:

- double negatives, for example, 'it was not impossible to foresee the consequences...'

- long words

- a complicated sentence construction

- technical jargon and other features that you may think look professional but in fact just get in the way of understanding and actually lessen the impact of your message.

The aim is to ensure that your reader progresses smoothly through the document, without having to stop and puzzle out what you are trying to say. As well as keeping it simple, it is useful to keep it short, and this may require some discipline and firm editing. Think about how long it takes to unravel a sentence such as the following:

It is our opinion that, in the circumstances, and with all things considered, the best way forward will be to talk initially to HQ, RSB and GRE staff, then JPU, EN and PNU staff about the new procedures and make sure that they are up to date.

If the author of this example is so unconfident about the way ahead, why should you, as the recipient, be convinced? Also, as the recipient, will you instantly recognise all the staff modules referred to? Is it the staff or the procedures that need to be up to date?

Style tips checklist

♦ Avoid long sentences or paragraphs

♦ Use simple, active language

♦ Avoid double negatives

♦ Avoid jargon or overuse of acronyms and abbreviations

♦ Use bullet points and numbered lists to break up the text

♦ Edit ruthlessly – don't hang on to a nice phrase that adds nothing just because you thought of it and like it.

In verbal communication, what you say is often not as important as the way you say it, and the message communicated to the recipient may have little to do with the actual words used. In written communications too, the tone you use may be so inappropriate as to be unacceptable, even if the facts it contains are true. Common errors are being:

♦ aggressive rather than assertive – 'I want this revised and on my desk by 8.30am tomorrow – or else.'

♦ patronising – 'I realise that your experience of this process isn't as extensive as mine. However...'

♦ dismissive – 'This is too trivial to comment on. Just go away and sort it.'

♦ critical – 'That was really stupid.'

Before you send a document, check it by putting yourself in the receiver's shoes. How would you react to being on the receiving end of it?

Other good practice

If the message is clearly set out, does it matter if you make minor errors, break the odd grammatical rule or misspell words? Think about how you would feel if your bank got your name wrong or a brochure for a smart hotel contained basic typing errors. You may feel that these small mistakes undermine the message the company is trying to convey. The key issue here is reliability. The message you receive is that if these people can't take the trouble to get the basics right, what else can't they be bothered to do, and what does that say for their levels of customer care?

These days, most typing and some grammatical errors can be picked up automatically by your spellchecker, but text will still benefit from proofreading to ensure that errors such as 'their' instead of 'there' are corrected, and that all personal names in the document are spelled correctly.

> **Politeness and clarity will get you a long way.**

You also need to keep a lookout for discriminatory language. This pitfall has been around long enough for acceptable alternatives to become current, for example 'workforce' for 'manpower'.

Be careful how you use numerical data in written communications. Incorrect numbers, or statistics provided out of context, can completely undermine your otherwise convincing case.

Presentation

You never get a second chance to make a first impression. If you are preparing a formal report or proposal, take care with the way it is set out and the kind of supporting material it might be useful to include. If, for example, your report contains lots of detailed information that will only be useful to some readers (or, because of its quantity and detail, will actually get in the way of your message) put this in an appendix.

Whatever the length of the document, it should be very easy for the reader to scan through it quickly and get the gist of what it is about. For a short document, that will mean short paragraphs (perhaps numbered) and sub-headings where useful – they will guide the reader quickly through the document content. A longer document requires a greater degree of formality. For a report or proposal, this will mean a title page and table of contents before the body of the document. Don't forget to put a date on it, and if the document will be going through several drafts, give it a version number as well. Make use of headers and footers: they are useful document identifiers, particularly if you have loose sheets in hard copy. Include your own contact details in case any covering letter gets separated from the main document. List appendices in the table of contents.

Sample report format

- ◆ Title page
- ◆ Table of contents
- ◆ Executive summary
- ◆ Introduction

◆ Methodology and findings

◆ Conclusions and recommendations

◆ Appendices

Activity 11
Evaluate written communications

Objective

This activity will help you to assess the clarity of your written communications.

Task

1 Select a paragraph or two (about 400 words) from a report or long memo that you have written.

2 Evaluate it against the style checklist below, using 1 for a low score and 5 for a high score. What conclusions do you draw from your evaluation?

Style checklist
Does the writer of this text:

◆ avoid long sentences that are difficult to follow?	☐ ☐ ☐ ☐ ☐ 1 2 3 4 5
◆ use simple, active language?	☐ ☐ ☐ ☐ ☐ 1 2 3 4 5
◆ avoid double negatives?	☐ ☐ ☐ ☐ ☐ 1 2 3 4 5
◆ use minimal jargon?	☐ ☐ ☐ ☐ ☐ 1 2 3 4 5
◆ use bullet points/lists (when appropriate) to break up the text?	☐ ☐ ☐ ☐ ☐ 1 2 3 4 5
◆ use appropriate punctuation, sentence structure and spelling?	☐ ☐ ☐ ☐ ☐ 1 2 3 4 5

Conclusions:

3 Now evaluate the following text using the same style checklist below.

> The traffic into London was heavy and it was almost two hours before I parked outside our apartment building. I had thought about it on the way, and I expected him to be there, but seeing him waiting for me as I got out of the car gave me a jolt to the heart. I paused before I crossed the road. He had taken up a position by the entrance where I would have to walk by him. He looked dressed up – black suit, white shirt buttoned to the top, black patent shoes with white flashes. He was staring at me, but his expression told me nothing. I walked towards him quickly, hoping to brush right by him and get indoors, but he stood across my path and I had to stop or push him aside. He looked tense, possibly angry. There was an envelope in his hand.

Source: *McEwan* (1997)

Style checklist
Does the writer of this text:

◆ avoid long sentences that are difficult to follow? □ □ □ □ □
1 2 3 4 5

◆ use simple, active language? □ □ □ □ □
1 2 3 4 5

◆ avoid double negatives? □ □ □ □ □
1 2 3 4 5

◆ use minimal jargon? □ □ □ □ □
1 2 3 4 5

◆ use bullet points/lists (when appropriate) to break up the text? □ □ □ □ □
1 2 3 4 5

◆ use appropriate punctuation, sentence structure and spelling? □ □ □ □ □
1 2 3 4 5

Conclusions:

Feedback

Fiction doesn't always have to be more interesting than fact. A style that is easy to read can be used to catch the reader's interest and sustain it.

Using the power of text in presentations

When you give a presentation, you are formally presenting a problem or a report in a structured way in a face-to-face setting. Just like written documents, a presentation is also an exercise in persuasion, since you are trying to get your audience to accept the message you are delivering to them. You may want them to take a particular course of action as a result of your presentation, or to accept your point of view or modify their own attitudes. Whatever you want from them, it is often the case that your need for their acceptance and approval is greater than their need to hear your message (Jay and Jay, 2000). It makes sense, therefore, for every element of the presentation to help in commanding the audience's attention and in ensuring a positive response to what you have to say.

Planning your presentation

The first element in planning your presentation is to get quite clear what your objective is, and to write this out in one sentence. For example, it might be 'to persuade senior management of the need to review our current customer relationship management system' or 'to present a case for switching resources from product x to product y'. The very fact of having to formulate a written statement will help to clarify exactly what you want, and provide a focus for you to check against as your presentation develops.

Now switch your attention to the audience. How interested, knowledgeable or confrontational are members of your audience likely to be? This will affect the points you want to make and how you propose to put them over. The next steps are as follows:

1   Write down how many sections or topic areas you need to cover, and the key points in each.

2   Note what is really important to get across, and what can be dropped or cut back if there is no time to cover it.

3   Devise some logical order for presenting the different sections. The usual structure is to start with some scene setting, go on to specific issues and end with an indication of what action is required next.

4   Put a notional time allocation against each section.

Did you know...?
Psychologists have plotted the attention span of an audience over a 40-minute period. It starts high, drops quite shallowly for the first 10 minutes, then more steeply until it reaches its lowest point after about 30 minutes. Then, with the end in

sight, it starts to rise again. Make sure you're not making your key point when your audience is at its least receptive!

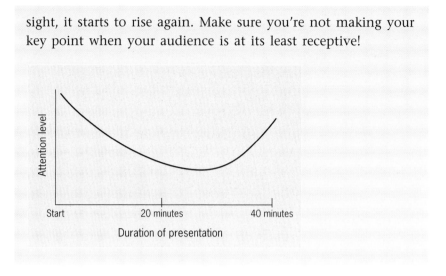

Source: *Jay and Jay* (2000)

Written script or cue cards?

Of course, the very best presenters dispense with notes altogether. They get to their feet or stride onto the podium and hold the audience enthralled with the power of their oratory. Alas, few of us ever achieve this admirable performance. The fact is that spontaneity is hard work, and being a relaxed and engaging presenter requires considerable preparation – not to mention a lot of self-confidence.

Less experienced speakers, or those giving short presentations to colleagues, can use cue cards (small index cards are ideal) on which the main points they want to make (or just key words) are listed. You will still need to prepare (in fact your preparation may need to be even more thorough), but it does mean that you stand a better chance of coming across as natural, and you have the assurance of a discreet written prompt if you suddenly go blank.

If you are a very inexperienced speaker, or the importance or formality of the occasion is one where you just can't afford to fluff your words, a written script can be reassuring. However, unless you're actually giving a lecture, DON'T turn a presentation into one. There is nothing more boring.

All the general principles of good written communication – keep it simple, clear, direct and jargon-free – also apply to a presentation. However, the difference here is that you are speaking not writing, and written and spoken language are very different. The challenge is to make your written script sound as if you are talking through the situation – better to use it as an extended crib rather than slavishly reading out each word.

Preparing notes for a presentation

◆ Use a less grammatical style: 'What are we doing this for?' rather than 'For what purpose are we doing this?'

◆ Write shorter sentences: run a 'comma check' to see whether there are phrases that can be cut altogether or split off to form separate sentences. If you tell your audience, 'Whatever the analysts say, in my opinion, if we go about things in the right way, there is no reason why, by this time next year, we should not come into profit,' you will have them yawning, even if the message is optimistic.

◆ Pose rhetorical questions – these require no answer but are useful for grabbing attention and sowing the seeds of an idea: 'Here we are with bulging order books and plant that keeps breaking down. So where do we go from here? Well...'.

◆ Use summaries and introductions to reinforce your message: 'We've just seen how...what I'd now like to do is look at...'

Time how long each section takes (including the time it takes to talk through any slides or other visuals) by speaking, rather than reading, the presentation. This should be done at normal speaking speed (with pauses for dramatic effect as appropriate!). Note down the timings of key sections in your script and monitor them – they will help to stop you running out of time before the end – and also insert references to slides in your script (in large print or a different colour) to provide useful triggers.

Designing and using text slides

Some experts argue that although 'a picture is worth 1,000 words', text slides (where you are giving the audience words rather than visuals) are a waste of time.

Slides should never be a substitute for a good presentation, but can provide the means of bringing it to life with some punchy bullet points. You do need to follow the basic rules though.

Arguments against text slides

◆ They distract the audience's attention from what you are saying

◆ If the slide is just repeating the points you are making, why are you bothering with it?

◆ People listen at the same rate, but read at different rates.

Arguments for text slides

- ♦ They provide a useful support and reinforcement for a presentation, not least because they can capture your key points in summary

- ♦ If they are also given to your audience as handouts, they can be used for note taking during your presentation, and can be taken away and mulled over later.

Slides that succeed

Do keep them short and snappy (think advertising slogans, think T-shirts) with no more than five or six points per slide.

Do make them big enough to read. PowerPoint (the standard Microsoft Office presentation software) is formatted automatically; if you use Word for overhead transparencies (OHTs), aim for headings of around 18 point and text at 16 point, using bold and italic for emphasis.

Do check each slide to make sure it really is adding value; if not, bin it.

Do use a maximum of one slide per three minutes of formal presentation time.

Do use them to break up the texture of your presentation and to add impact and interest to it.

Do provide a low-tech back-up (for example a set of OHTs) in case of technical problems.

Do check that the technology is in place for displaying your slides (and the back-up if necessary) and that you know how to use it. Have a dry run in advance in the presentation venue if possible.

Don't be so distracted by the slides you take your eyes off the audience; you're presenting to people, not a screen. Print off a hard copy that you can keep in front of you.

Don't produce slides from tables of figures; no one will be able to read them, so be ruthlessly selective with numerical data.

Don't (unless you are very experienced) try lots of fancy stuff, with text and graphics whizzing in from all directions.

Don't produce slides of diagrams where text is set at different angles.

Don't overcrowd slides with more text and graphics than viewers can take in easily.

Using a video conference to make your presentation

If you are making your presentation to a remote audience using video-conferencing facilities you will probably modify your approach accordingly.

You may have access to an autocue system. If you do, find out what arrangements need to be made so that you can use it for your presentation. You will need to receive some guidance, training and practice in using it beforehand.

In video conferencing you are on camera. The equipment is usually low contrast and low resolution – which you should bear in mind when choosing what to wear. Because of the remote transmission there is often a gap between speaking and receiving – similar to long distance telephone calls, so you need to be more deliberate in the way you converse with people. The following tips for using video conferencing should help you to prepare to deliver your presentation remotely.

Video conferencing tips

♦ You should not have to worry about technical details – IT staff should set up the equipment, adjust cameras, sound and lighting. IT staff will also put away equipment etc. at the end of the conference. Check that they will be available for the time the conference is scheduled.

♦ If you are using PowerPoint slides during the presentation, make sure that all participants will be able to receive these. It may not be feasible to use these for the presentation.

♦ Circulate any documentation in advance, including any outline of the presentation and any PowerPoint images that you may want to deliver during the presentation.

♦ Brief the chairperson in advance about what to expect from your presentation – for example time, interaction with audience, outline of coverage.

♦ Wear pastel shades; avoid white and black; and use plain clothes without patterns.

♦ Arrive early for the conference so that you can settle in, get acquainted with the equipment, set-up and seating arrangements.

♦ Have a glass of water to hand during the conference.

♦ Begin the video conference with a sound check and camera check for all participants and make sure everyone is settled in before getting down to business.

- Most conferences are booked for a predetermined amount of time – make sure your presentation fits within the time allocated, allowing for two-way discussion.

- Sit up or stand so you can breathe and speak normally.

- Talk at a normal rate, pitch and tone. The microphone means you don't need to raise your voice.

- Make the presentation interactive: it is easy for a remote audience to switch off – watch out for signs of this among your audience such as not attending or fiddling – and pose questions or invite comment to keep the audience engaged.

- Allow for the slight delay in the transmission of video and audio when asking for questions or contributions from the audience. For example, do not rush the conversation and allow a contribution to end before initiating a new input.

- Do not interrupt another person as this will cut them off mid-sentence.

- Remain seated (or standing if this is the arrangement) so that the camera can stay trained on you. Have documents to hand so that you don't have to reach across a desk or go off-camera. Try to avoid white paper; you could use a coloured folder to hold your documents.

- If you feel a coughing fit coming on or need to discuss something off camera, use the mute button.

- Think about what action you want from participants, for example feedback on your ideas. You may want to invite them to think about an issue and circulate their ideas on it after the conference.

Source: *Adapted from University of Cambridge Computing Service* (1998)

◆ Recap

Identify the features of clear written communication

- Most documents are written for a purpose, for example to persuade or to inform. The first step in writing an effective document is to define what you want to achieve and what you want your readers to do.

- Information within the document should be presented so that it meets the needs and interests of your readers and is easily accessible. The most important information should be presented first.

Evaluate your writing style

- Effective business communication should:
  - avoid sentences that are difficult to follow
  - use simple, active language
  - avoid double negatives
  - use minimal jargon
  - use bullet points/lists (when appropriate) to break up the text
  - use appropriate punctuation, sentence structure and spelling.

Plan an effective presentation

- Be selective about what you include in a presentation. Focus on making a few really important points that will enable you to achieve your aim and will interest the audience.

- Shape these into a presentation structure that sets the scene, explains the issues and concludes by telling people what action is required next. Present keys points when the audience is most alert – at the start and end of the presentation.

Develop notes and visual aids to support your presentation

- Develop notes as a memory jogger for when you deliver your presentation but avoid writing a script. Small index cards that list the main points or key words are ideal.

- Use slides to reinforce your presentation and bring it to life. There are arguments for and against using text slides. If you do use them, follow the guidance in the 'Slides that succeed' checklist.

 **More @**

Walters, L. (2002) *Secrets of successful speakers*, **McGraw-Hill**
This is an excellent book for anyone wanting to develop their skills as a presenter.

Leigh, A. (1999) *Persuasive Reports and Proposals*, **Chartered Institute of Personnel and Development**
This handbook covers five crucial aspects which spell out the word 'PRIDE' – what you should feel about your documents if they are to win hearts and minds: Purpose, Readers, Image, Detail and Enhancers.

Strunk, W. and White, E. (1999) *The Elements of Style*, **Allyn & Bacon**
This classic text shows you how to be clear, concise and precise, and is itself written in a similar style.

Try the communications skills directory of **Mind Tools** at www.mindtools.com for advice on communicating in writing and on presentation skills.

Information systems

So far in this book we have focused on how you can improve your own management of information. But you are working within an infrastructure of organisational information and knowledge systems.

This theme explores the key issues in systems development and reviews how the Internet is transforming corporate communication systems. The massive growth in computer systems and the use of Web-based technology have attracted a corresponding rise in the number and variety of threats to security. With widespread desktop access to e-mail and the Internet, all managers – indeed all staff – need to be alert to the dangers of unauthorised access to an organisation's systems.

In this theme you will:

- ◆ **Identify the key stages in the system development life cycle and your contribution towards it**
- ◆ **Identify the benefits of an corporate intranet**
- ◆ **Assess how well your organisation manages data security.**

Key issues in systems development

It's a fair guess that many of your working hours are spent in front of a computer, using the information system in different ways: reading, inputting, organising and sending out data. Typically, there will be times when the system won't do what you want it to do, or you think, 'Why did they design it like this? Why can't I just go straight to... It's useless...' However, the way your system was designed probably originally depended (at least to some extent) on the way local users and managers described the jobs they wanted the system to perform. This legacy will have a crucial impact on the way you manage your own incoming and outgoing information and, by extension, the extent to which the organisation as a whole manages and makes accessible its information and knowledge resources.

At some point in your career you will be involved in providing input to a major system upgrade or replacement, even if you have not yet done so. Understanding how and why systems are developed, and the possible pitfalls, provides important lessons for managers involved in future systems development.

Systems model and life cycle

Computers have been with us for a long time, but their development has been surprisingly unpredictable. Up until the 1970s there were few attempts to produce a coherent view of computer operations. One of the first models was developed by Richard Anthony (Mason and Willcocks, 1994). This was actually a model of organisational behaviour, which put forward the view that there are three basic types of decisions made within organisations:

- ◆ **Strategic:** these involve setting overall goals and objectives and determining how to meet them

- ◆ **Control:** making sure that the organisation's functions are carried out efficiently and resources are used effectively

- ◆ **Operational:** relating to day-to-day operations, ensuring that tasks are done properly, in the right order, at the right time.

As a model, Anthony's pyramid (see Figure 4.1) has had a huge influence on management thinking – and will still be recognisable in your own organisation today. This hierarchical view of functions within the organisation was mirrored by the systems managers' approach, which was geared to the belief that the logical starting point for introducing computer applications was at the operational level, working upwards from there to the rarefied heights of supporting strategic business decisions.

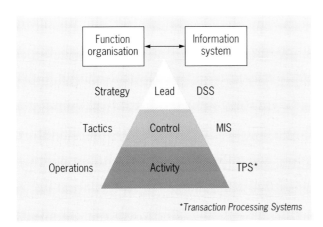

Figure 4.1 *Anthony's pyramid*   Source: *Mason and Willcocks* (1994)

From the late 1960s it was realised that systems development actually consisted of well-defined stages, and a 'life cycle' view of systems emerged that formed the basis of many different methodologies for systems development (Galliers et al. 1999). Even so, it took a long time to realise that the life cycle was not linear, with a neat start and end point, but needed to be viewed as a continuing process in order to:

- ◆ review and correct earlier errors and misconceptions

- ◆ revisit and retune the original specification in the light of changing requirements

- ◆ deal adequately with the problem of a growing number of systems involving increasing amounts of maintenance.

Figure 4.2 gives a graphical view of a system life cycle.

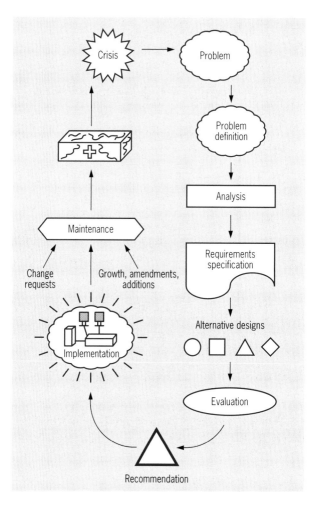

Figure 4.2 *The system life cycle*   Source: *Mason and Willcocks* (1994)

Your role in developing information systems

If you are not an IT manager, where do you fit into this process? You may not realise how important you are. Recent years have seen the growth of user involvement at every stage of systems development. As the impact of systems development has become visible and organisation wide, organisations have belatedly realised that it has a human dimension, and that ignoring this can wipe out all the advantages of your expensive new system.

Many organisations are now battling with the problem of so-called legacy systems. This is a system that was developed 20-odd years ago which was designed to solve the problems the organisation faced at that time. The trouble is that 20 years on, they are out of step with evolving business needs and can hold back organisations that want to apply a more up-to-date set of routines. They are now seen to be inflexible, expensive to maintain and even more expensive to replace. This has all lent urgency to the need for genuine user involvement in systems design, and few would dispute the necessity for this. But mistakes still happen. Lytle (1991) devised an information systems development disaster menu, shown in Figure 4.3, that still holds good. As you can see, it shows all the things you shouldn't do when developing computer systems. If you do, then you're heading for disaster.

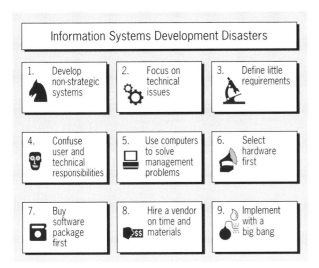

Figure 4.3 *An information systems disaster menu*   Source: *Lytle* (1991)

Let's turn the negatives from Figure 4.3 around and see what happens.

1 **Develop strategic systems.** What are the key *strategic information areas* for your business? These are your key business critical systems.

2 **Don't focus on technical issues.** Systems are not a matter of hardware and software; they are a matter of the *right* hardware and the *right* software, selected on the basis of user needs and organisational critical success factors.

3 **Take time to define requirements at 'big picture' and operational levels.** This is a key area of a manager's job. Welcome it as a real opportunity to examine quite critically what you are doing now. Do you still need to do it at all? Are there other, better ways of achieving your objectives? This will involve you in the following activities:

◆ Analysing all the business processes that you manage. For example, if you're an HR manager, this will include such areas as recruitment, appraisal and reward, workforce planning and job analysis and design. How do the functions that you manage fit into the wider organisational picture?

◆ Documenting the type of information you need to carry out your various tasks. Are you receiving everything you need, in the most efficient and timely way? Are you getting too much information, information you don't need at all or need less often?

♦ Drawing a picture of the data that flows in and out of your unit (don't forget to include informal data sources). What, and from where, are your data feeds? Who else receives the same information? What do you do with the information you receive? If you process it in some way, how is this done and what are the outputs? Who are they delivered to?

4 **Be clear about user and technical responsibilities.** Make sure that responsibilities are clearly defined at the outset, with staff allocated the roles that they are best qualified to do. That way you can build up co-operation and mutual respect, not mutual antagonism.

5 **Use management, not computers, to solve management problems.** Too often, problems that are actually related to poor management are conveniently blamed on 'the system'. Computers can do lots of things to improve your data management and information flow, but they can't resolve problems of organisational culture or personality clashes. Do what you can to get these issues resolved before your user specification gets underway.

6, 7 and 8 **Select hardware and software to fit the requirement, and be specific about any customisation required.** Adopt the motto 'focus on functionality'. Vendors are experts at showing off their systems to their best advantage, but will the system do what you want it to do? Can the software be customised, and will the vendor do this? Will they need to involve third-party suppliers? If customisation is required, get this specified in terms of activities and costs. Hiring on a time and materials basis is a recipe for a long drawn out, expensive and increasingly sour relationship.

Find out when the next version of the software is due. What do the licensing arrangements really mean in terms of multiple, real-time access? It is important to check out the vendor's financial stability as a standard procedure, and it may also be worth checking the business press to see whether the company (or its parent) is involved in merger discussions or is about to be swallowed by a giant competitor.

9 **Beware 'big bangs'.** It is rare now for a complete system to be developed in full before live operation, and for good reason. It takes time to develop a complete system, and while this is happening there will inevitably be evolution and change in user requirements. These need to be incorporated into the developing system and checked by the user to see if they work. It is much better to develop a prototype system that can be piloted (tested, reviewed and improved) and used to inform the final development.

Intranets and extranets

The idea of getting computers to communicate with each other, either on a one-to-one basis or via a network, has been around for a long time. Networks are of two main types, determined by the size of area that they cover:

◆ **Local area network (LAN)** which can link computers in a single room, one building or several buildings that are geographically close (for example on a university campus)

◆ **Wide area network (WAN)** which, as its name implies, can link computers that can be hundreds or even thousands of miles apart.

The widespread take-up of the Internet in recent years has transformed the way that networks are used, and added a whole new dimension (with new opportunities and new problems) to the way in which organisations communicate internally and externally.

An **intranet** is a network (LAN or WAN) that utilises Internet technology. However, unlike the Internet, access to an intranet is restricted to specific individuals, and the data it holds will be secured behind stringent data security systems or firewalls.

An **extranet** uses Internet technology to link together intranets in different locations. In contrast to intranet transactions, extranet transmissions take place over the Internet, and so are not secure. This necessitates strengthening the security of the connecting portions of the Internet. This can be done by creating 'tunnels' of secured data flows. The Internet with such tunnelling technology is known as a virtual private network (VPN) – see Figure 4.4.

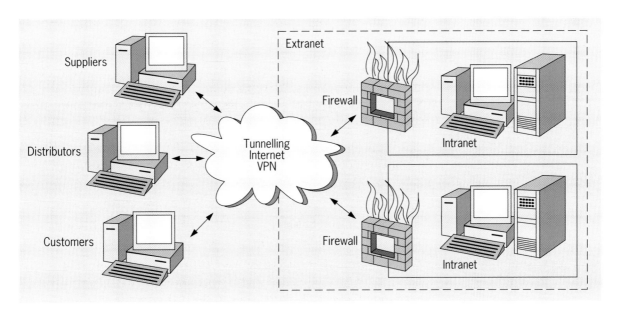

Figure 4.4 *Diagrammatic contrast of the Internet, intranet and extranet*

Source: *Turban et al.* (2000)

Both systems and departmental managers have been quick to seize the advantages of a corporate intranet:

With businesses under significant pressure to empower employees and to better leverage internal information resources, intranets furnish a very effective communications platform – one that is timely and extensive. A basic intranet can be set up in days and can eventually act as an 'information hub' for the whole company… Intranets can provide the following features:

♦ easy navigation (internal home page provides links to information)

♦ ability to integrate a distributed computing strategy (localised web servers residing near the content author)

♦ rapid prototyping (can be measured in days or even hours in some cases)

♦ accessible via most computing platforms

♦ scaleable (start small, build as requirements dictate)

♦ extensible to many media types (video, audio, interactive applications)

♦ can be tied to 'legacy' information sources (databases, existing word processed documents, groupware [software designed for group communication and shared group use]).

Source: *Shim (2000)*

The potential business benefits of intranets are numerous (Fishenden, 1997):

♦ improved information flows between employees, customers and suppliers

♦ reduced geographical constraints: worldwide organisations can now communicate as a logical whole

♦ easy access to information through a common single interface

♦ better access to information = quicker and better decision making = reduced cost

♦ reduced cost of IT operations: Internet-derived technology is a cheap way of improving communication and data flows

♦ increasing an organisation's profile on an international scale: selected components of an intranet can be shared via a public interface on the Internet.

It can be used for a huge range of practical applications, from making corporate information available to all employees to providing specific information to a salesforce in the field or external stakeholder groups.

Albion Oil
Having secured a contract to assist with exploration and exploitation of natural resources in North Africa, Albion Oil needed a means of handling its rapidly growing information assets and communicating efficiently with all members of a project team scattered across Europe, North Africa and North America. A technical review of the existing infrastructure revealed a mix of Macs, PCs and UNIX systems. What to do? These are the steps they took:

- Produced a project initiation document defining key business objectives

- Restricted the scope of the project to users involved in the North African exploration

- Defined key deliverables, including the establishment of a user group

- Defined key success criteria – e.g. providing users with reliable and secure access to information and round-the-clock support and training

- Documentation, clarification of roles and responsibilities and mechanisms for addressing security, reliability, contingency and other issues were all established as necessary targets

- Clear targets were identified in terms of 'publishing' information (authoring, formats, ownership), locating information and Newsgroup 'netiquette'

- The project was controlled by a small tightly focused team

- Beginning with an online telephone directory of staff as a pilot, Albion moved to adopt the same approach to other project related data. The results have been a system that matched management and user requirements in which the technology was clearly focused and not just applied for its own sake.

Source: *Fishenden* (1997)

Activity 12
Identify useful content for your intranet

Objectives

Use this activity to:

◆   identify useful content for including on your intranet

◆   evaluate your organisation's intranet from a user's point of view.

Task

1   If you have an intranet, note down in the first column of the chart a selection of the content currently available on it (for example staff directory, training information, minutes of particular committees, product or project information).

2   Next note down whether you regard this information to be a useful facility or not, and why.

Content example	Useful or not?	Why?

3   If your organisation does not have an intranet, what would you like to have available on one? What benefits would you expect to accrue from this?

What content?	Expected benefit?

Feedback

What you learned from this activity will depend on whether your organisation has an intranet or not and, if it does, how well you rate it. If you have identified significant strengths, are there ways you can capitalise on them that you have not yet explored? If you have identified obvious weaknesses, why not put your ideas forward? If, on the other hand, you have considered what you would like to have available on an intranet, you may find it helpful to discuss the benefits you aim to achieve with a colleague or friend.

Data security

Security threats can present themselves in direct form, through hackers (and as far back as 1997 it was estimated that the Internet is hacked into every 20 seconds) and through indirect information systems penetration (Mitchell et al. 1999). These indirect threats occur in four major types:

◆ **Worms:** a worm is a program that, once established, can spread copies of itself throughout a network

◆ **Trojan horses:** these are also programs that appear to be carrying out a non-malicious activity which, when activated, reveal their true destructive intent

◆ **Logic bombs:** these are programs activated by a specific event, for example St Valentine's Day

◆ **Viruses:** like a medical virus, these 'infect' other programs.

A popular route in for these invaders is via e-mail – and they don't always come in as attachments. The header message is usually friendly and intriguing, encouraging the user to believe that it is a message from a friend or admirer.

The results of these attacks can range from the irritating and embarrassing to the devastating, and can include the destruction of data or its modification, interception or fabrication by unauthorised personnel.

The Melissa virus
Melissa was an e-mailed virus that emerged from nowhere to overwhelm commercial, government and military computer systems, leading the FBI to launch the biggest Internet manhunt ever.

Melissa affects Word 97 and Word 2000 documents. If launched, this virus will attempt to start Microsoft Outlook to send copies of the infected document to up to 50 people in Outlook's address book as an attachment.

The e-mail subject line reads:

Important message from [username]

While the message reads:

Here is that document you asked for ... don't show anyone else. ; –)

Source: *MelissaVirus.com* (www)

Viruses often spawn ever more dangerous variants. The 'I Love You' virus, which appeared in Spring 2000, had 50 variants by October that year.

The growth of e-commerce has seen a surge in opportunities for business fraud and other security issues.

KPMG survey
The management consultancy firm KPMG has produced some worrying findings from its 2001 *Global e-fr@ud Survey*:

♦ E-fraud is a growing problem for companies around the world.

♦ Although credit card numbers and personal information are of prime concern to customers, less than 35 per cent of companies surveyed have had security audits performed on their e-commerce systems.

♦ 50 per cent of businesses identified hackers and poor implementation of security policies as the greatest threats to their e-commerce systems. However, the company is at greater risk of being the victim of an internal security breach.

♦ 83 per cent of respondents feel that the public perceives the traditional 'bricks and mortar' business as more secure than e-commerce-based dot.coms.

Source: *Adapted from KPMG* (2001)

Methods of data security

There is a range of methods of varying complexity that organisations can use to protect themselves from unauthorised access. See Table 4.1.

Method	Description
Firewalls	The first line of defence from the outside. Acts as a security guard for the company's internal network, filtering all incoming traffic from the Internet. A good tool for networks connected to the Internet
User authentication	Verifies the identity of the user. Could also be used to restrict access to certain resources within the network. A requirement for any user accessing a corporate network
Data encryption	Scrambles the data before and during transmission. Use this method when data protection is important
Key management	Acts like a 'key' to access encrypted data. Maximum protection to protect data from unauthorised parties. Use in conjunction with data encryption
Digital certificate	Like a watermark on a bank cheque – this is an electronic ID card that establishes your credentials when doing business on the Web
Intrusion detection system (IDS)	Scans the network for abnormal activity and security breaches. A minimal requirement for any corporate network
Virus detection	Scans the network data for viruses, providing both prevention and cure if updated regularly. One of the best defences for data protection
Virtual private networks (VPN)	A secure private data network developed on a public data network like the Internet
Extranets	A secure private data network that uses a public data network like the Internet to extend a company's network to suppliers, vendors, partners, etc. A company can minimise its overheads by exchanging data through an extranet via electronic data interchange (EDI)

Table 4.1 *Methods of data security*   Source: *Hawkins et al.* (2000)

Data protection

Another aspect of information security is data protection. One of the effects of increasing globalisation of business activities and cross-border data transactions has been to raise awareness of the need to safeguard personal details which are held in either manual or electronic systems. Several basic principles of data protection have now been established and codified in law. For example, in the UK, anyone processing personal data must comply with the enforceable principles of good practice. These are that personal data (which includes facts and opinions, and information regarding the intentions of the holder of the data towards the individual) must be:

◆ fairly and lawfully processed

◆ processed for limited purposes (for example legitimate business purposes)

◆ adequate, relevant and not excessive

◆ accurate

◆ not kept longer than necessary

◆ processed in accordance with the data subject's rights

◆ secure

◆ not transferred to other countries without adequate protection.

To find out more about data protection requirements, you could do an Internet search for your country using key words 'data protection'. A useful site for UK-based managers is www.dataprotection.gov.uk, where these principles can be found.

Every organisation, whether government, public or private sector, needs to devise its own specific security arrangements. The following provides a useful checklist of good practice in information security management.

Good practice in information security management

♦ Draw up a security policy document

♦ Allocate specific security responsibilities

♦ Institute security awareness and training programmes for staff

♦ Have a formal reporting procedure for security incidents, and make sure that staff are aware of it

♦ Implement good antivirus controls, updated daily (a problem here can be with mobile staff who spend a lot of time on the road and forget to update)

♦ Identify risks to business operations and develop disaster plans

♦ Control proprietary software copying – make sure that only software developed by or licensed to the company is used

♦ Safeguard organisational records to protect them from loss or falsification

♦ Comply with your country's data protection legislation and ensure that the information you record is only used for general business purposes

♦ Monitor compliance with security policy throughout the organisation and review arrangements periodically.

Source: *British Standards Institution* (1995)

Activity 13

Assess how well your organisation manages data security

Objective

Use this activity to check out your department or organisation's information security management.

Organisations are increasingly vulnerable to unauthorised and damaging access to their systems. Being aware of potential risks can enable them to forestall many problems by good data management and contingency planning.

Task

1   Complete the questionnaire below and try to answer the questions honestly. You may like to consult with colleagues over any 'don't knows'.

My department/organisation has the following:	Yes	No	Don't know	Comments
A security policy document	☐	☐	☐	
Security responsibility which is specifically allocated	☐	☐	☐	
Security awareness training for all staff	☐	☐	☐	
A formal, well-known reporting procedure for security incidents	☐	☐	☐	
Good continuous security controls	☐	☐	☐	
Identified risks to business operations and drawn up contingency plans	☐	☐	☐	
Rigid control of software copying	☐	☐	☐	
Well-protected organisational records	☐	☐	☐	
Compliance with current data protection legislation	☐	☐	☐	
Regular monitoring and review of security policy compliance	☐	☐	☐	

Feedback

If you don't know about your organisation or department's security policies, you should find out. Do your IT colleagues know more? The key point is that security is everyone's responsibility. Managers can help to raise awareness of the risks and take action to make sure that the organisation and its departments have established contingency plans and have adopted good practice for the security of the information that they manage.

◆ Recap

Identify the key stages in the system development life cycle and your contribution towards it

◆ Systems pass through a series of stages during their development; problem definition and analysis, specification of requirements, design and evaluation of options, recommendation and implementation.

◆ Systems development should be seem as cyclical rather than linear. Maintenance is required on an ongoing basis to manage change requests, growth, amendments and additions.

◆ User involvement is critical at each stage of the life cycle if the system is to meet its purpose and be fit for use.

Identify the benefits of a corporate intranet

◆ Intranets utilise Internet technology and have become a very popular means of improving information flow and communication through an organisation.

◆ Access is restricted to authorised individuals and data is secured behind firewalls, making intranets a safe and cost-effective approach to networking.

◆ An effective intranet should have directories and search engines that make it easy for users to find and retrieve the information that they need. Achieving this level of user friendliness requires careful planning.

Assess how well your organisation manages data security

◆ Security threats present themselves directly from hackers and indirect threats of four major types: worms, viruses, Trojan horses and logic bombs.

◆ Data can be made more secure through the use of firewalls, user authentication, data encryption, key management, digital certificates, intrusion detection systems, virus detection software, virtual private networks and extranets.

♦ Organisations should minimise the risk to their data by designing and implementing data security and management policies.

▶▶ More @

Wilson, D. (2002) *Managing Information: IT for Business Processes*, Butterworth-Heinemann
This book provides a compelling rationale for organisations to use information management systems and for individuals to acquire the skills to manage and use the systems.

Cobham, D. and Curtis, G. (2004) *Business Information Systems: Analysis, Design and Practice*, Financial Times Prentice Hall
This book provides a comprehensive understanding of how information systems can aid the realisation of business objectives, covering topics from systems, design analysis and planning to data mining, business intelligence and knowledge management.

The online library **BetterManagement** at www.bettermanagement.com provides free articles and white papers on a whole range of management topics including information technology. Select LIBRARY.

You can access the Data Protection Act at **Her Majesty's Stationery Office** – www.hmso.gov.uk/acts/acts1998/19980029.htm

5 Knowledge management

Knowledge management has been hyped as a must-have business solution for a number of years now. However, quite what it is and how you are supposed to manage something so intangible is still a source of much confusion.

In this theme you will:

♦ **Define knowledge management and its relationship to learning processes**

♦ **Identify the barriers to knowledge management**

♦ **Identify the critical success factors in knowledge management**

♦ **Mobilise knowledge management in your organisation.**

How do you manage knowledge?

One of the problems in trying to define knowledge management is that it is sometimes difficult to see how it differs from information management. Swan et al. (2000) see the two as being very closely associated, with each interacting with the other. See Figure 5.1.

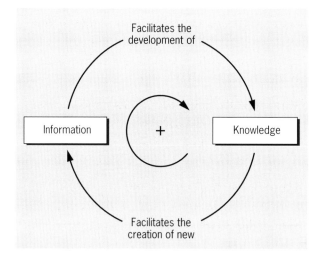

Figure 5.1 *The dynamic relationship between information and knowledge*

Source: *Swan et al.* (2000)

As explored in Theme 1, knowledge combines information, experience and insight into something that is unique to every individual. But what is knowledge management? Here are two definitions:

Knowledge Management is the **explicit** and **systematic** management of **vital knowledge** and its associated **processes** of creating, gathering, organising, diffusion, use and exploitation. It requires turning personal knowledge into corporate knowledge that can be widely shared throughout an organisation and appropriately applied.

Source: *Skyrme* (www)

Or, put another way:

Knowledge Management...has been described as 'knowing what you know, knowing what you don't know, learning what you need to know and sharing it.'

Source: *Newing* (2000)

It is worth being aware that different disciplines are concerned with recognising, valuing, capturing and measuring the knowledge and expertise within organisations, and adopt a range of terminology. Intellectual capital, for example, is a term that is often used alongside knowledge management. It has a broader definition than knowledge and comprises employees' talent and knowledge, customer loyalty, the value of brands, patents and copyrights and research. In this theme we focus on the concept of knowledge management given in the definitions from Skyrme and Newing above.

The concept of knowledge management grew in the early 1990s from a study of how Japanese companies create knowledge within the organisation, disseminate it and embody it in new products and services (Nonaka and Takeuchi, 1995). The Nonaka and Takeuchi model classified human knowledge into two kinds:

Explicit knowledge: this is formal, easily identifiable and general knowledge, the sort you find in mathematical expressions, or specifications and manuals. Because it is explicit and obvious, it can easily be transmitted between individuals.

Tacit knowledge: this is difficult to articulate, as it is personal, 'hidden' knowledge, embedded in an individual's experience and coloured by their personal beliefs and values.

These are the two basic building blocks of knowledge creation. The assumption is that knowledge is created through the dynamic interaction between explicit and tacit knowledge. For organisations to succeed, they need to find ways to make explicit and share the wealth of tacit knowledge that is locked up within individual employees' experience. Nonaka and Takeuchi saw the explicit/tacit relationship as a spiral process, in which interaction takes place repeatedly. Willard (1999) reworked and simplified their original spiral (see Figure 5.2), and sees the sequence in this way:

♦ Someone has a bright idea, and finds a way (sometimes easily, sometimes with great difficulty) of expressing that idea. This means that the idea moves from the *tacit* (personal knowledge and experience) to the *explicit* – expressed in a way that everyone can understand.

♦ The person who had the idea combines this with other known elements to form some kind of context (so we have *explicit* added to *explicit*).

♦ This is then communicated to colleagues, who begin to 'get the picture' and start to think about it on the basis of their own knowledge (so the *explicit* idea moves to *tacit* reflection and analysis).

♦ Through discussion the idea grows and develops, and colleagues all contribute to the implicit understanding that builds up (adding *tacit* to *tacit*).

♦ New ways are found to express the idea, more people are informed and the idea is increasingly combined to present a bigger idea (and so on).

♦ The new understanding is now institutionalised – turned into a working procedure or implemented as a working practice or rule.

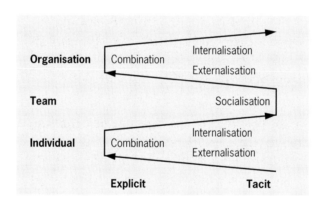

Figure 5.2 *The knowledge spiral*   Source: *Willard* (1999)

Much of the literature about knowledge management relates to the technology: the systems for sharing and exploiting the newly explicit knowledge. However, knowledge management is actually about people and their interaction, rather than technology – though technology is a powerful enabler.

Knowledge management and learning

An important aspect of knowledge management is the way people (and organisations) learn and how they approach problem solving. This is a good point to revisit Argyris and Schön's theories-in-use (the private, self-generated theories that govern our behaviour).

Argyris and Schön (1974) built a model of the processes involved in the theory in practice (see Figure 5.3) that has three elements:

♦ **Governing variables (or values):** there are likely to be a number of these and any action taken is likely to impact on them.

♦ **Action strategies:** what people do to keep their governing values within an acceptable range.

♦ **Consequences:** what happens as the result of an action. Consequences can be intended or unintended.

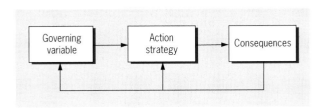

Figure 5.3 *Theory-in-use model*   Source: *Smith* (2001)

Where the consequences of your action strategy are in accord with your governing values, the theory-in-use is confirmed. But what happens if the consequences work against your governing values?

Argyris and Schön suggest that there are two responses to this mismatch, which they describe as **single-loop learning** and **double-loop learning**. When something goes wrong, a common response is to look for another strategy that will work better, but still within the framework of existing governing variables or values – the plans, goals or rules of behaviour that we are familiar with. This is single-loop learning. A more radical approach is to examine critically the governing variables or values themselves, to test how valid they still are. This in turn can lead to a change in the whole framework in which the action strategies and consequences are developed – a double-loop (see Figure 5.4).

How does this translate into organisational learning and behaviour? Looked at in organisational terms, error and correction in a single-loop learning environment will work within the organisation's existing policies and objectives, but otherwise carry on with these unchanged. Double-loop learning will occur when errors are corrected in ways that involve the modification of the organisation's underlying norms, policies and objectives. Argyris and Schön argue that double-loop learning must be maximised if organisations are to make informed decisions in rapidly changing contexts. It is an approach which accords very well with the underlying values of knowledge management.

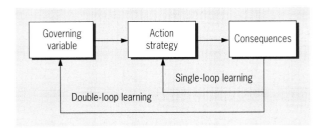

Figure 5.4 *Double-loop learning*   Source: *Smith* (2001)

If you're still wondering what use knowledge management is, take a minute to think about the following case study.

Case study

A specific example of this corporate amnesia can be found at Ford, where new car developers wanted to replicate the success of the original Taurus design team. But no one remembered, or had recorded, what was so special about that effort... The assumption that technology can replace human knowledge or create its equivalent has proven false time and again.

Source: *Davenport and Prusak* (1998)

Business benefits of knowledge management

Several business benefits have been identified as accruing from knowledge management (Newing, 2000):

◆ identifying new markets from high-level intelligence gathering and pooling of knowledge by experts

◆ more responsiveness to market needs by harnessing external knowledge

◆ using customer knowledge to improve existing products and create innovative new ones

◆ faster time to market

◆ better quality products

◆ reusing knowledge gained in other parts of the world for other customers with similar problems

◆ continuous learning and development of best practice

◆ reducing costs associated with finding and reinventing knowledge by quickly retrieving explicit knowledge already stored

◆ improving customer service by applying knowledge at the point of first interaction with the customer

◆ reduction of risk by using wider expertise.

Of all the initiatives we've undertaken at Chevron during the 1990s, few have been as important or as rewarding as our efforts to build a learning organization by sharing and managing knowledge throughout our company.

Source: *Derr* (www)

Accepting the theory, and acknowledging the benefits, is a good starting point. But there can be considerable challenges and problems, which we will look at next.

Challenges and critical success factors

As a concept, knowledge management can involve some fundamental rethinking about the value of individual knowledge, and how the retention or sharing of knowledge by individuals is perceived and rewarded by the employing organisation. The argument runs: 'If knowledge is power, why should I diminish (or eliminate) my power base by sharing it?' This is one of many challenges that management faces in introducing knowledge management. Here we examine some of the key issues and the critical success factors.

Barriers to knowledge management

Even if your organisation has taken on board the message that using your corporate knowledge more intelligently can be a vital component in competing in the marketplace, it may well face a number of basic problems before it can get underway (Bonaventura, 1997). There may be, for example:

- no model for knowledge creation and dissemination within the organisation: you've never done it before so where do you start?

- no processes or systems focused on supporting those activities – they weren't part of the original systems specification so where do they fit in now?

- no systems able to measure or evaluate how well you are creating and disseminating knowledge

- no means of evaluating the effectiveness of the knowledge creation and dissemination activities that you are carrying out.

Von Krogh et al. (2000) believe that managers ought to be supporting knowledge rather than trying to manage it, as it is basically unmanageable and not amenable to traditional management techniques. Individual staff may be reluctant to accept new lessons, insights and ideas, and many organisations can be quite challenging places for people learning to overcome the barriers of sharing knowledge with others. Individual barriers can include the following:

- People approach new experiences on the basis of their experience and beliefs about the world. There will be some situations which are so new and different that they will not have developed a response to them, and will find them too challenging.

♦ Some people will see new knowledge as a threat to their self-image, and respond negatively to it.

The organisation itself may contain its own barriers:

♦ New ideas will have to be made explicit in a 'language' that people in the organisation can understand

♦ The organisational memory and understanding of how things work can be good for bonding people together – but also make it more difficult for an individual to disagree with a 'party line'

♦ Organisational procedures may make cross-functional interactions difficult.

Key questions for management

Bonaventura (1997) describes how, where there are no existing models on which knowledge creation processes and systems can be based, management will typically just issue a general call for more 'learning'. This will fail, because the organisation will not have in place the reporting structures, compensation mechanisms or procedures that are necessary to support it, or because they don't understand the knowledge creation and knowledge dissemination process, and think it can be managed just like everything else. Bonaventura puts forward some questions for the management of any organisation (particularly those in the knowledge intensive sectors of the global economy) to ask of itself:

♦ What do our culture and our actions as managers say about the value of knowledge in the organisation?

♦ How is knowledge created, embodied and disseminated? What is the relationship between knowledge and the kind of innovation that we need to achieve our objectives?

♦ What commercial benefits do we expect to gain from more effective knowledge management?

♦ Where are we in terms of the maturity of our knowledge systems?

♦ What role does IT play in our knowledge management programme?

Skyrme (1998) has identified a number of recurring characteristics within organisations that demonstrate best practice in knowledge innovation, which also translate into key questions for management:

1   Is your knowledge strategy separate or clearly linked to your business strategy?

2   How much is knowledge discussed in your organisation, and how well is it understood? Is it a key element in your plans and budgets?

3   Is the knowledge facet of your business articulated as a real, compelling vision? Is there a framework that guides management decisions?

4   Are there knowledge champions throughout your business? Does your chief executive officer (CEO) link the importance of your organisational knowledge to your business success?

5   Do you have systematic processes for capturing, organising and sharing knowledge throughout your organisation?

6   Are people and information readily accessible through your computer and communication networks? Do these networks extend to customers, suppliers and experts?

7   Do you measure the contribution of knowledge to your organisation's performance?

Only when an organisation has realistic answers to these questions can it start to develop real advantage from its knowledge assets.

The employee perspective

So much for management – but what about the staff? As Morling (2000) points out, asking or telling employees to 'share knowledge' is a waste of time. It may look good in the strategic plan, but won't on its own satisfy the needs of staff to feel valued and recognised for their contribution. For an employee, the benefits of knowledge management relate less to organisational performance than to the general human desire for interaction with other people and some kind of shared interest or expertise within quite small groups, where opinions and ideas are freely exchanged, respected and trusted.

These small groups of shared interest or expertise (knowledge 'communities') can fulfil a useful role by creating a balance between the enterprise on the one hand and the individual on the other. A common mistake that management makes in trying to implement knowledge management is to focus on the individual as the source of knowledge – somebody who can deposit a 'knowledge package' of their expertise and experience into the system for use by all. This fails to recognise the role of collaboration in developing ideas, or that for many people the real reward of sharing knowledge is the immediate response from the people they have shared it with.

Morling's company, has developed a system of 'communities', defined as:

> ...a group of people sharing a common interest or practice, whose purpose is to share knowledge and experiences, help each other to learn, act as a support network and sometimes as an informal centre of excellence.

Source: *Morling* (2000)

The knowledge and skills gained in the community can be applied directly to the needs and issues of the organisation through the members' formal organisational roles and participation in teams. For example, they can be used as a specific project team, or within a geographical sales division. The point is that they become a seeding ground for new ideas, competencies and skills. Here is a summary of the basic principles:

The seven Cs of communities

Context – the community sets the context for knowledge sharing and creation

Contribution – members know where and how to contribute

Creation – knowledge is created through the interaction of members

Collaboration – members collaborate to build on each other's ideas

Consensus – members agree on best practices and how to take ideas forward

Content – knowledge is captured as reusable content

Capitalisation – the organisation can exploit new knowledge and best practices.

Communities do need a certain amount of nurturing to develop. If you've identified a potentially useful knowledge community within your organisation, here are some tips to get it working to good effect:

♦ Identify a core group of people with the motivation and commitment to get it started

♦ Make sure that the group has a leader who can manage the context of the community, so that when the context shifts the community can respond like a team would

♦ Hold regular meetings

♦ Enlist management support

♦ Ensure access to appropriate technology

♦ Give the group self-governance

♦ Pay attention to team building, especially by helping new members of the community to feel welcome and comfortable and able to participate actively and constructively.

Activity 14
Assess your organisation's attitude to knowledge management

Objective

Use this activity to assess what your organisational culture says about the value of knowledge within the organisation.

Task

Read through the questionnaire provided. For each question, tick the response that applies most closely to your own organisational situation.

1 What do our culture and our actions as managers say about the value of knowledge in the organisation?

   a The value of knowledge is openly discussed and the organisation actively encourages knowledge sharing ☐

   b There is a lot of talk about knowledge management but it is difficult to see any real benefit from it so far ☐

   c The present management structure and reward systems are geared to individual knowledge and expertise ☐

2 How do we create and disseminate knowledge?

   a There is a clear and explicit relationship between knowledge and innovation in new product and service development ☐

   b We have some useful shared databases but there is no obvious link that I can see to the innovation process ☐

   c We're not sure what this 'knowledge' is or how it could be useful to us ☐

3 Do we recognise the commercial benefits of knowledge management?

   a The commercial benefits of knowledge management are well recognised and we are clearly aware of the value of our intellectual property assets ☐

   b There is a view that some time could be saved by sharing more information around the organisation, but this is not so substantial that we would give it priority ☐

   c We have not identified any clear benefit for our organisation of adopting a knowledge management approach ☐

4 How mature are our knowledge systems?

   a We are constantly looking for new ways to use our systems in order to make the most of our knowledge assets ☐

   b We have an intranet with a staff 'Yellow Pages' and some other databases, but they don't seem to be updated very often so nobody uses them ☐

   c We don't see the need for this kind of organisation-wide system. We get all we need from our separate systems for payroll, marketing, etc. ☐

5   What role does IT play in our knowledge management programme?

a   It is seen as an essential enabler, but uses input from across the organisation to develop   ☐
     improvements to systems

b   The IT department thinks it should be responsible for everything to do with systems and gets   ☐
     quite defensive about too much input from other departments

c   IT drives our knowledge management programme   ☐

Feedback

If you have mostly ticked a, your organisation is well on the way to making full use of knowledge management, and may be an example of best practice in its own sector. If you have mostly ticked b or c, use this activity as an opportunity to reflect on how far the organisation is 'unfriendly' to knowledge management. How far do you personally believe it has real business value?

Knowledge management in practice

Theory is one thing, practice quite another. How do you get from a grand vision to operational reality? How do you start to mobilise the static knowledge held within your organisation? Some of the world's most successful companies have adopted a knowledge management approach as the best way to maximise the value of their own knowledge assets and to build good strategic partnerships and customer relations. Many of them have been more than ready to share their experiences via documented case studies. Some of these are included in this section. Here we set out some practical stages in getting underway when setting up a knowledge management programme.

Approaches to knowledge management

Skyrme (1998) reports that in analysing the way that over 100 organisations apply knowledge management, two main approaches have been identified:

◆ **Sharing** existing knowledge so that organisations don't reinvent the wheel because the knowledge they need is available but not known to them. For example, a department of the US giant AT &T spent US$79,449 to obtain information that could have been found in a publicly available document from their associate company Bell Research for US$13.

◆ **Creating** new knowledge and converting it into new products, services and processes, enabling better, faster innovation. Jaguar is one company that has focused on this. By codifying how the best engineers design a particular car body panel, engineers can develop detailed designs in hours rather than weeks. This meta-knowledge – analysing how professionals go about their work – is becoming an important facet of a firm's knowledge that needs to be captured and shared.

Source: *Skyrme* (1998)

Skyrme found that in both approaches, organisations tend to focus on a few knowledge 'levers' to strengthen their knowledge-building efforts:

◆ **Customer knowledge** – develop deep knowledge-sharing relationships, and understand the needs of your customers' customers

◆ **Stakeholder relationships** – improve knowledge flows between suppliers, employees, shareholders

◆ **Business environment insights** – systematically scan your political, economic environment, etc. and monitor what your competitors are doing

◆ **Organisational memory** – share knowledge through best practice databases, directories of expertise, intranets

◆ **Knowledge in processes** – embed knowledge into business processes and management decision making

◆ **Knowledge in products and services** – surround products with knowledge, for example in user guides and knowledge-intensive services

◆ **Knowledge in people** – set up innovation workshops, learning networks, communities of knowledge practice.

The knowledge created within an organisation must add value (Tissen et al. 1998). If the creation of knowledge is to be successfully directed, then the people involved in it must be too. Here are some examples:

Pharmaceuticals company Hoffman-LaRoche is using the approach of knowledge domains and knowledge links in order to reduce its time to market. It has calculated that each day gained in market availability represents a monetary gain of US$1m.

CIGNA Property & Casualty, an insurance company, has created an 'upward value spiral' for know-how to be shared through the company. Employees' information and knowledge is processed by 'knowledge editors' and distributed throughout the organisation.

Source: *Tissen et al.* (1998)

Procter & Gamble is a consumer-products giant with nearly 110,000 employees spread in locations across the world. Aware that its success depended in part on the knowledge locked in the minds of its employees, P&G used knowledge-sharing software to transform departmental experts into tangible information resources for the whole company. In particular, scientists and engineers working in numerous locations across the world could benefit from collaborating and sharing information and expertise.

The company's intranet was found to be 'doing a good job connecting people to knowledge that was documented and published, but not as good a job in connecting them to experts', commented Mike Telljohann, associate director at P&G's technical centre in Cincinnati. He explained that it was clear people did not know where to go with questions. They suspected that there was knowledge out there that they couldn't access.

In response to this feedback the company introduced an integrated system from AskMe Enterprises that forms a directory listing of individuals noted as subject-matter experts who can be called on to lend advice or collaboration for problem solving and product development. It provided a single knowledge base in the company. But a key advantage of the system was that it was able to reward active participants – 'the more active you are in a particular area, the software highlights you as a featured expert. People in the innovation area enjoy being seen as an expert – it gives a lot of personal satisfaction.' Telljohann and his team spent a lot of time marketing the benefits of the system. But return on investment from the pilot project was enough to persuade the company to invest in large-scale implementation.

Telljohann sums up the benefits: 'I think the experts feel like they can make more of an impact. They typically have close circles they share experiences and knowledge with; this broadens their ability to share what they know, and the people with questions have a place to go.'

Source: *Adapted from Moore* (2001)

Here are some other practical projects that organisations can undertake to improve their knowledge management:

- ◆ Create knowledge databases of best practice, expertise, client profiles, legislative developments
- ◆ Create a knowledge map (a visual representation of information and relationships)
- ◆ Actively manage processes for collecting, classifying, storing and disseminating information
- ◆ Develop knowledge centres that are focal points for specific knowledge, and knowledge webs – networks of experts
- ◆ Introduce collaborative technologies like intranets or groupware
- ◆ Appoint a senior executive to be responsible for the knowledge initiative.

Source: *Skyrme* (2000)

Steps to knowledge mobilisation

To summarise, let's try and pull together all the different aspects of making the most of knowledge assets. Paul Miller (1998) provides a good overview of the process which he calls 'knowledge mobilisation', shown in Figure 5.5.

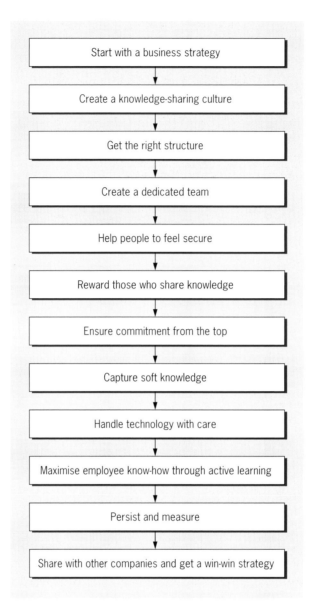

Figure 5.5 *The 12 steps to knowledge mobilisation*

Source: *Adapted from Miller* (1998)

Let's look at these steps in more detail, with examples provided by Miller (1998) that illustrate how some organisations have put theory into practice:

1   **Start with a business strategy** – before you start changing things, you must understand the business strategy to which knowledge mobilisation can contribute.

2   **Create a knowledge-sharing culture** – easier said than done! But if your culture is one that says 'knowledge is power' and your pay and benefits system rewards the hoarding of knowledge, then the system has to change. Remploy, which specialises in employing disabled staff, has introduced critical paths to make its employees more proactive in knowledge sharing.

3   **Get the right structure** – flatter organisational structures (rather than many hierarchical levels) encourage knowledge sharing.

4   **Create a dedicated team** – changing culture is a major initiative and needs a dedicated team to push it forward. This team will raise the knowledge profile and publicise the organisation's commitment to knowledge sharing. Ernst & Young recognised that it had cultural obstacles to overcome, arising from its traditional culture of not sharing knowledge in order to protect client confidentiality. It set up a large team of knowledge workers to drive initiatives forward and monitor the results.

5   **Help people to feel secure** – employees don't willingly share knowledge if they feel their jobs are under threat, and organisations must acknowledge this.

6   **Reward those who share knowledge** – knowledge contributions need to be recognised in the pay structure. At Boston Consulting Group, a part of each consultant's compensation depends on knowledge mobilisation activities.

7   **Ensure commitment from the top** – the role of the CEO is essential to culture change. Employees need to see top management promoting knowledge sharing if they are expected to do so.

8   **Capture soft knowledge** – connect people with people, and create multilevel networks to capture soft knowledge. Sun Microsystems brings together its employees worldwide by job function on a regular basis to train them in developments in the company and the market.

9   **Handle technology with care** – technology can enable knowledge mobilisation, but it's useless without the necessary culture.

10 **Maximise employee know-how through active learning** – cascade learning throughout the organisation – cross-functional knowledge sharing increases awareness of roles and responsibilities. Allen & Overy's junior lawyers present their experiences and areas of expertise to new entrants; partners give presentations at other levels. There is a continuous process of learning.

11 **Persist and measure** – when people leave, they take their training and know-how with them. Organisations need to capture that knowledge.

12 **Share with other companies and get a win-win strategy** – be open to the idea of sharing non-sensitive information with other companies.

Activity 15
Explore good practice in knowledge management

Objective

Use this activity to explore good practice in knowledge management within an organisation that has adopted it.

Task

1 Access the BP website at www.bp.com

2 Explore the main sections of the site. What clues are provided in these sections that the organisation has embraced the principles of knowledge management?

Clues provided on BP's website:

3 Finally, compare the style, tone and the kind of information and facilities provided on this website with your own organisation's website – if there is one.

Comparisons:

Feedback

An organisation's website is its public face – what it projects to the world. If you delve into BP's site, you may note the following points:

◆ BP's stand on a range of key issues, such as social/ethical, environmental and employee issues

◆ the wide range of information about the company's activities that is made available to customers (and employees)

◆ initiatives for the wider community including education services and a schools link

◆ the company's customer focus, and the image it projects.

Based on the site as viewed December 2004

Although BP doesn't use the term 'knowledge management', it has embraced the principles of knowledge management, especially in the way that it shares knowledge and facilitates communication among people throughout the organisation.

The company has also been used in a case study of knowledge management. For further information see: www.kmresource.com/exp_cases.htm

Your comparisons with your own organisation's website will depend on your organisation's openness and how much information it is prepared to share, and on how user or customer focused it is.

◆ Recap

Define knowledge management and its relationship to learning processes

◆ Knowledge management is a technique for codifying tacit knowledge, and for making it widely available in the organisation.

◆ Despite being seen as a technology-based technique, knowledge management depends for its success on the ability of people in the organisation to acquire new knowledge through learning.

◆ Double-loop learning supports dissemination of knowledge. It occurs when an error is detected and corrected in a way that involves modifying the organisation's underlying norms, policies and objectives, enabling the organisation as a whole to benefit from the learning.

Identify the barriers to knowledge management

♦ There are challenging barriers to knowledge management.

♦ Individuals may see knowledge management as a threat to their powerbase or they may lack the experience or context that enables them to acquire new knowledge in a particular situation.

♦ Organisations may not recognise the value of their knowledge assets or may not have the culture, language or processes in place to support the creation and dissemination of knowledge.

Identify the critical success factors in knowledge management

♦ Knowledge management is a strategic process that needs to be aligned with other elements of business strategy, compensation mechanisms, the reporting structure and the technology processes that are necessary to capture and disseminate knowledge.

♦ Collaboration through knowledge communities is an effective way to encourage sharing and development of personal knowledge.

Mobilise knowledge management in your organisation

♦ There are 12 steps in Miller's (1998) knowledge mobilisation precess – see figure 5.5.

 **More @**

Nonaka, I. and Takeuchi, H. (1995) *The Knowledge-Creating Company: How Japanese Companies Create the Dynamics of Innovation*, Oxford University Press
This is a classic text revealing how Japanese companies translate tacit to explicit knowledge and use it to produce new processes, products and services.

Wenger, E., McDermott, R. and Snyder, W. (2002) *Cultivating Communities of Practice*, Harvard Business School Press
Another highly reputable text arguing that while knowledge communities do form naturally, organisations need to become more proactive and systematic about developing them and integrating them into their strategy.

Gorelick, C., April, K. and Milton, N. (2003) *Performance Through Learning: Knowledge Management in Practice*, Butterworth-Heinemann
This is a practical guide to the key issues surrounding knowledge management from a human resource perspective and it provides

incisive insights into developing a strategy linked to organisational learning.

www.kmresource.com/exp.htm is an excellent knowledge management gateway that provides links to a selection of reviewed sites and/or resources.

References

Argyris, C. and Schön, D. (1974) *Theory in Practice: increasing professional effectiveness,* Jossey-Bass

Argyris, C. (1999) On Organisational Learning, Blackwell Publishers

Bawden, D., Holtham, C. and Courtney, N. (1999) 'Perspectives on information overload', *Aslib Proceedings,* Vol. 51, No. 8, 249–255

Bonaventura, M. (1997) 'The benefits of a knowledge culture', *Aslib Proceedings,* Vol. 49, No. 4, 82–89

Bradley, P. (1999) 'Efficiency in Numbers', *Information World Review,* May

British Standards Institution (1995) *Code of Practice for Information Security Management (BS7799)*

Buckley, P. and Clark, D. (2004) *A Rough Guide to the Internet,* Rough guides

Clifton, H. D. (1990) *Business data systems*, Prentice Hall

Cobham, D. and Curtis, G. (2004) *Business Information Systems: Analysis, Design and Practice*, FT Prentice Hall

Cooke, A. (1999) 'Neal-Schuman authoritative guide to evaluating information on the Internet', *Searcher: the Magazine for Database Professionals,* June, pp.22–31

Data Protection Act 1998, The Stationery Office Ltd, www.hmso.gov.uk/acts/acts1998/19980029.htm

Davenport, T. H. and Prusak, L. (1998) *Working knowledge: how organisations manage what they know,* Harvard Business School

Dawson, A. (1997) 2nd edition, *The Internet for Library and Information Service Professionals,* Aslib

Derr, K. quoted in The Knowledge Management Resource Center site at www.kmresource.com/exp_cases.htm

Edmunds, A. and Morris, A. (2000) 'The problem of information overload in business organisations: a review of the literature', *International Journal of Information Management, 20,* 17–28

European Forum for Electronic Business, www.eema.org

Fishenden, J. (1997) 'Managing intranets to improve business process', *Aslib Proceedings,* Vol. 49, 4, April, pp.90–96

Galliers, R. D., Leidner, D. E. and Baker, B. S. H. (1999) 2nd edition, *Strategic information management: challenges and strategies in managing information systems,* Butterworth-Heinemann

Gorelick, C., April, K. and Milton, N. (2003) *Performance Through Learning: Knowledge Management in Practice,* Butterworth-Heinemann

Hawkins, S., Yen, D. C. and Chou, D. C. (2000) 'Awareness and challenges of Internet security', *Information Management and Computer Security*, Vol. 8, No. 3, 131–143

Horton, F. W. and Lewis, D. (1991) *Great information disasters*, Aslib

Information Management Report (2000) Bowker, May, 4

Informix (1999) 'Executive Summary', www.informix.com

Jay, R. and Jay, A. (2000) *Effective presentation*, Prentice Hall

Kolb, D. A. (1985) *Learning styles inventory*, McBer & Co

KPMG (2001) *Global e-fr@ud Survey*, www.kpmg.co.uk

Leigh, A. (1997) *Persuasive reports and proposals*, Chartered Institute of Personnel and Development

Lytle, R. (1991) 'The PPS information systems development disaster in the early 1980s', in Horton, F. and Lewis, D. (eds.) *Great information disasters*, Aslib

Mason, D. and Willcocks, L. (1994) *Systems analysis, systems design*, Alfred Waller Ltd

McEwan, I. (1997) *Enduring Love*, Vintage

MelissaVirus.com, www.melissavirus.com

Miller, P. (1998) *Mobilising the power of what you know: a practical guide to successful knowledge management*, Century Ltd

Mitchell, R. C., Marcella, R. and Baxter, G (1999) 'Corporate Information Security Management', *New Library World*, Vol. 100, No. 1150, 213–227

Moore, C. (2001) 'Tapping Knowledge', 12 October, www.infoworld.com

Morling, J. (2000) 'Share or else', *Consultants' Advisory*, December, 30–32

Newing, R. (2000) 'Knowledge economy', *Consultant's Adviser*, Iss. 3, 2–4

Nickerson, R. C. (2001) 2nd edition, *Business and information systems*, Prentice Hall

Nonaka, I. and Takeuchi, H. (1995) *The Knowledge-Creating Company: How Japanese Companies Create the Dynamics of Innovation*, Oxford University Press

Reuters (1996) *Dying for information*, Reuters Business Information

Shim, J. K. (2000) *Information systems and technology for the non-information systems executive*, St Lucie Press

Simpson, C. W. and Prusak, L. (1995) 'Troubles with information overload', *International Journal of Information Management*, Vol. 15, No. 6, 413–425

Skyrme, D. (1998) 'Developing a knowledge strategy', *Strategy*, January, 18–19

Skyrme, D. (2000) 'Knowledge Management: making it work', www.skyrme.com

Skyrme, D. 'Knowledge Management: making sense of an oxymoron', www.skyrme.com

Smith, M. K. (2001) 'Chris Argyris: Theories of action, double-loop learning and organizational learning', *The encyclopedia of informal learning,* www.infed.org/thinkers/argyris.htm,

Strunk, W. and White, E. (1999) *The Elements of Style* Allyn & Bacon

Swan, W., Langford, N., Watson, I. and Varey, R. J. (2000) 'Viewing the corporate community as a knowledge network', *Corporate Communications*, Vol. 5, Pt. 2, 97–106

Tissen, R., Andriessen, D. and Deprez, F. L. (1998) *Value-based knowledge management*, Addison Wesley Longman

Turban, E., Lee, J., King, D and Chung, H. M. (2000) *Electronic commerce: a managerial perspective*, Prentice Hall

University of Cambridge Computing Service (1998) Technical User Services, 23 October, www.tus.csx.cam.ac.uk/videoconf/vctips.html

Von Krogh, G., Ichijo, K. and Nonaka, I. (2000) *Enabling knowledge creation: how to unlock the mystery of tacit knowledge and release the power of innovation,* Oxford University Press

Walters, L. (2002) *Secrets of successful speakers*, McGraw-Hill

Wenger, E., McDermott, R. and Snyder, W. (2002), *Cultivating Communities of Practice,* Harvard Business School Press

Willard, N. (1999) 'Knowledge Management: foundations for a secure structure', *Managing Information*, June, 45–49

Wilson, D. (2002) *Managing Information: IT for Business Process*, Butterworth-Heinemann